Cricut Cutting

The Ultimate Cricut Book Collection V1, 2 & 3

How to Master Your Cricut Machine

Maryann Gillespie

ISBN-13: 978-1729777930

ISBN-10: 1729777937

Table of Contents

Introduction to Cricut Tips

My name is Maryann Gillespie, and I love my Cricut. I couldn't always say this, though. For the first several weeks I fought with my machine and spouted some very unpleasant words in its direction. I was tempted to box it up and put it in the closet along with a few other craft machines I've purchased through the years.

But then I started to learn a few tricks. These slight tweaks changed my experience from frustrated to pleasurable.

I've been a crafter for several years. I slaved over intricate baby books for my children. I became a crafter on steroids making sure everyone in the family got tons of cute, artsy-fartsy creations.

One of the breakthroughs in my crafting expertise was purchasing my Cricut machine. Once I mastered it the possibilities were endless.

I currently use the Cricut Expression, and I'm thrilled with everything it does. Not only do I use it for my scrapbooking but also a host of other crafting projects.

I don't even remember the last time I purchased a greeting card. I could never be happy with boxes of store bought cards again.

A few of my favorite projects include using vinyl to make wall art and personalizing my kid's toys and practically everything else in their rooms. I'm sure you have a long list of your favorite Cricut project ideas too.

The Cricut can be used to cut paper, vinyl, fabric and a bunch of other stuff. You can cut letters from an assortment of fonts as well as thousands of graphic images. You're truly only limited by your imagination.

You'll find yourself walking through department stores looking at expensive decorative pieces and thinking "I can make that at home using my Cricut."

If you ever need inspiration for new craft projects just go to Pinterest and view the projects others have posted. Looking through these will get your own creative juices flowing into high gear.

I love my Cricut because it allows me to use my creativity in so many different ways.

However, I've talked to many other women who are still unhappy with their machines. They've never gotten past the annoyed phase.

They become frustrated when their machine messes up or doesn't work properly. So they pack it back into the box and stuff it in the closet. I hate to see that happen.

Not only have these folks spent their hard earned money on an unused machine - but I hate to see the potential of these machines being wasted. I know these crafters would love what they create with their Cricut if they could just master a few tricks and techniques.

I want to help others learn to enjoy their Cricuts as much as I do. It was this desire to help others that inspired this book.

I am not a high-tech person. I'm only telling you that so you'll know if I can learn to use a Cricut so can you. I didn't start with any special knowledge or skills, just the desire to create fantastic artwork that could be shared with my family and friends. I have even sold items at craft fairs and farmer's markets.

My hope in writing this book is to help you enjoy your machine and to kiss the frustration good-bye!

Here are a few of the things we'll be learning about in this book:

The pros and cons of the different Cricut machines.

How to choose which Cricut to purchase based on your needs.

Finding the proper settings for specific materials.

How to troubleshoot problems you encounter with your machine.

Do the risks outweigh the benefits of buying used Cricut products?

Ways to save money on supplies.

Do it yourself repairs.

Plus a host of other ideas, tips and troubleshooting techniques to help you conquer your machine. By the time you finish reading this Cricut book for dummies, you'll be using your die cutter for an assortment of projects.

My goal is to help you learn from some of my mistakes so you can save yourself a lot of time and money. You'll also make some amazing artwork along the way.

Let's get started.

Chapter One - Cricut Machines and Troubleshooting Techniques

I want to start by explaining the differences in the most popular Cricut machines. If you haven't yet bought your Cricut, it might help you decide which model you need.

They each have their pros and cons so I can't tell you one is definitely better than the other. They have various capabilities and different price points.

Cricut Personal, Create and Expression

These machines do not require a computer to work. They have their own LCD screen display and keyboard. The designs are programmed using cartridges. If you want to be able to use your machine without connecting to a computer, then this is a good option. Each cartridge contains around 700 images, so you get a multitude of choices with each one.

The Personal and Create machine cuts designs from 1 inch to 5 1/2 inches. (Make sure to read the Warranty Warning chapter to see which machines have been discontinued as this may influence your buying decision.)

The Expression machine can cut designs from 1/4 inch to 23 1/2 inches in size. You are able to orient the paper for landscape or portrait.

Usually, one font cartridge and one shapes cartridge comes with your machine.

Sometimes you can purchase a bundle with your machine that includes several cartridges at a discounted cost. There's also a chapter later in this book where I tell you about several ways to save on cartridges. You can often find them much cheaper if you know where to look.

These are older machines, and you can buy one used on Amazon or eBay if you want to save some money. I discuss the pros and cons of buying used machines in a later chapter.

Cricut Expression 2 Tricks

Version 2 is the newest model of the Expression machine, which is probably the most popular model among Cricuter's. You do not need a computer to use this machine. It has its own screen and keyboard, so you program your cuts without ever connecting to a computer.

However, when I'm going to be working on my Cricut for a while, I find working on the larger computer screen much more pleasant than the small LCD display. To work on the computer, you'll be using the Cricut Craft Room software by Provo Craft - the company that sells Cricuts. All the machines are compatible with the Craft Room, so to get the most functionality from the design software your need to download it and install it on your computer.

An advantage of the Expression 2 is that you don't need the keyboard overlays that were necessary with previous machines. You can see the images on the LCD screen.

This machine allows for a choice of portrait or landscape orientation. Design sizes can be as small as 1/4 inches and as large as 23 1/2 inches. A complaint I often hear is that the machine only comes with a 12 x 12 mat. It seems that if it does the larger cuts, it should come with a 12 x 24-inch mat also. But it must be purchased separately.

Cricut Mini Hints

This machine represents a significant change from the machines we just discussed. The biggest difference is this one requires being connected to a computer, Windows or Mac and an Internet connection. You can't use it without being connected to your computer and the Cricut Craft Room software.

Because it doesn't have its own built-in display or keyboard, it is much cheaper to purchase. This makes it a good option for someone who doesn't craft a lot or who wants to test the Cricut waters before making a larger investment.

Also, it is much smaller in size than the other machines. If you like to take your Cricut to crops or to fairs, it can be a good choice. But don't forget, you will need to take a laptop and have Internet access too.

It will take up less room in your house which is handy for those who don't have a dedicated craft space.

The mini will cut paper 8 1/2 by 12. This means the designs it cuts are from 1/4 inch to 11 1/2 inches. It will not cut large designs like the larger machines.

All cartridges are compatible with the Mini except for Imagine cartridges. This little bug even works with the Cricut Gypsy which is the portable handheld design studio.

Troubleshooting Techniques

I realize that no one wants to hear what I'm about to say, but it's important to mention it anyway. When you first get your machine, take some time and look through the user manual.

I know that the Cricut user manuals are not the best in the world. But at least follow the set-up guide carefully. Then look at the chapter on Basic Operations. After that, you can refer to the manual as the need requires. When you try something new then at least see what the manual has to say.

The keyboard and commands on the Cricut can seem overwhelming at first. You need to at least familiarize yourself with all the basic commands and icons. You can refer back to the manual later when you need to learn about a particular item.

The least you'll need to know is where to find the speed dial, pressure settings, blade depth, and load mat button.

The guide will walk you through calibrating your machine in the beginning to make sure it's lined up correctly.

Then you'll be given a test project to make your first cut. Follow the directions carefully. Enter each command slowly; the machine can freeze if you give it too many directions too quickly.

Also, read about your warranty. You need to know what your warranty covers, how long it lasts, and what will **void the warranty**. You don't want to do something accidentally that will prevent you from returning a machine that is broken and still under warranty.

This next section deals with some of the most common problems I hear users complain about. A lot of these troubleshooting techniques will work on multiple machines; others are machine specific.

Material Tearing or Not Cutting Completely Through

This is the biggest problem with most Cricut users. When this happens, the image is ruined, and you've wasted material. More machines have been returned or boxed up and put away due to this problem than any other.

But don't panic, if your paper is not cutting correctly there are several steps you can take to try and correct the problem. The problem could be a blade issue which we discuss in more detail in a later chapter. But I'll touch on a few things briefly in this section.

Most important is this: Anytime you work with the blade TURN YOUR MACHINE OFF. I know it's easy to forget this because you're frustrated and you're trying this and that to make it work correctly. But this is an important safety precaution that you should remember. And yes, I'll mention this again in the chapter dedicated to blades!

Make simple adjustments at first. Turn the pressure down one. Did it help? If not, turn the blade down one number. Also, make sure the mat is free of debris so the blade rides smoothly.

Usually the thicker the material, the higher the pressure number should be set to cut through the paper. Don't forget to use the **multi cut function** if you have that option. It may take a little longer to cut 2, 3 or 4 times, but by then it should cut clean through.

For those of you using the smaller bugs that do not have that option here is how to **make your own multi-cut function**. After the image has been cut, don't unload the mat just hit load paper, repeat last and cut. You can repeat this sequence 2, 3 or 4 times to ensure your image is completely cut out.

If you are using thinner paper and it is tearing try reducing the pressure and slowing down the speed. When cutting intricate designs, you have to give the blade enough time to maneuver through the design. By slowing it down it will be able to make cleaner cuts.

Another thing to consider when working with fancy, intricate cuts is if you've **chosen to cut the design too small.** You may have a hard time cutting it out, try increasing the size and see if that helps.

Clean the edge of the blade to be sure no fuzz, glue or scraps of paper are stuck to it.

Make sure the blade is installed correctly. Take it out and put it back so it's seated firmly. The blade should be steady while it's making cuts. If it makes a shaky movement it's either not installed correctly, or there's a problem with the **blade housing**. (To watch how to change blades see the video tutorial section.)

While the blade is out, make sure the housing is clear of any fuzz or debris. Take a piece of wire and clean out the hole in the blade housing or just blow in the hole to get rid of any fibers that collect in the housing. A little routine maintenance can go a long way in preventing cutting problems. **When you change the blade make it a habit to clean out the housing**.

Switch to a new blade. The problem may be as simple as a dull blade. If the blade is new, it could be a **defective blade**. I make recommendations about sharp, long lasting carbon blades in another chapter.

Be aware that there is a deep cutting blade for thicker material. You'll want to switch to this blade when you're cutting heavy card stock. This will also save wear and tear on your regular blade.

Cutting a lot of thick material will obviously wear your blade out quicker than thinner material and cause you to change it more often.

Occasionally the problem can be the paper itself. If you've bought cheap paper you might try the same cut with a higher quality paper and see what happens. Also, some card stock has a high fiber content that simply **makes clean cuts impossible**. If you run into this problem be sure and make note of where you purchased the product and the brand name. You don't want to make the same mistake again. Really thin paper can also be a problem.

You may need to tape the paper to the edges of the mat to keep it from slipping around during the cut. If the paper moves while it is being cut it is more likely to rip and tear.

Another big problem is having the settings incorrect for the type of material you're using. This can be confusing; especially when you're just learning the machine or you're working with a new kind of material. I have included a quick cutting chart in the resource section of this book.

Always make sure your mat has enough stickiness to hold the material still while it runs through the machine. We discuss mats in more detail in a later chapter.

Check that the mat has enough clearance as it leaves the machine. If it becomes blocked in any way the mat can be thrown off track.

There are various problems I hear about regarding mats especially involving their stickiness or lack of stickiness. We will discuss these in a later chapter.

Machine Freezing

I've talked to several crafters who say their machines freeze up occasionally.

Remember to always turn your machine off when you switch cartridges. When you switch cartridges leaving the machine on it's called "hot swapping" and it can sometimes cause the machine to freeze. This is more of an issue with the older models and doesn't seem to apply to the Expression 2.

You know how quirky electronic gadgets can be, so give your machine a rest for five or ten minutes every hour. If you work for several hours continuously, your machine might overheat and freeze up.

Turn the machine off and take a break. Restart it when you come back and it should be fine. Then remember not to rush programming the machine and give it an occasional rest.

Don't press a long list of commands quickly. If you give it too much information too quickly it will get confused in the same way a computer sometimes does and simply freeze up. Instead of typing in one long phrase try dividing up your **words into several cuts**.

If you're using **special feature keys** make sure you press them first before selecting the letters.

Power Problems

If you turn your machine on and nothing happens the power adapter may be at fault. Jiggle the power cord at the outlet and where it connects to the machine to make sure it's firmly connected. Ideally, you want to test the adapter before buying a new one. Swap cords with a friend and see if that fixed the problem. Replacement adapters can be found on eBay by searching for Cricut adapter power supply.

The **connection points** inside the machine may also pose a problem; here is how to test that. Hold down the plug where it inserts into the back of the machine and turn it on. If it powers up, then the problem is inside the machine and the connection points will have to be soldered again.

If the machine powers up but will not cut then try a hard reset. See the resource section for step-by-step instructions on resetting your machine.

Here are a few tips especially for Expression 2 users. Have you turned on your machine, you watch it light up and hear it gearing up but when you try to cut nothing happens? Or you're stuck on the welcome screen or the LCD screen is unresponsive.

Well here are two quick fixes to try. First try a hard reset sometimes called the **rainbow screen reset** to recalibrate your die cutter. If that does not resolve the problem you're going to have to restore the settings.

For step-by-step video instructions on resetting and recalibrating your Expression 2 (see the resource section for the link) and watch the video that solves your particular problem.

When using the Cricut Sync software to update your Expression 2 machine, you suddenly get error messages like the device is not recognized or not found, try using a **different USB port or temporarily disable your firewall or antivirus software as they may block the updates**. Remember to enable them when the updates are complete.

To help cut down on errors try to keep your machine updated. When an update is available, you should receive a message encouraging you to install the latest version.

For those of you using third party software that is no longer compatible with the Cricut you probably already know that **updating your machine may disable that software**.

When you cut heavy paper and your Expression 2 shuts down try switching to the normal paper setting and use the **multi cut function**.

Carriage Will Not Move

If the carriage assembly does not move, check to see if the **belt has broken or if the car has fallen off the track**. Provo Craft does not sell replacement parts, which is nuts, so try to find a compatible belt at a vacuum repair shop.

If the wheels have fallen off the track, remove the plastic cover and look for a tiny screw by the wheel to unscrew it. You now should be able to move the wheel back on track.

Unresponsive Keyboard

If you are sure you are pressing the keys firmly, you have a cartridge inserted correctly and a mat loaded ready to go, but the keypad is still not accepting your selection, the problem may be internal.

You will have to remove the keyboard and check if the **display cable is connected to the keypad and to the motherboard**. If the connections are secure then you have a circuit board problem and repairs are beyond the scope of this book.

An important reminder, please do not attempt any repairs unless your machine is out of warranty.

Weird LCD Screen

The LCD screen is now showing strange symbols or is blank after doing a firmware update. Try running the update again making sure your selections are correct.

When the image you choose is bigger than the mat or paper size you selected the preview screen will look **grayed out** instead of showing the image. So increase the paper and mat size or decrease the size of your image.

Also watch out for the gray box effect when using the **center point feature**. Move the start position down until you see the image appear. The same thing may happen when using the fit to length feature. Try changing to landscape mode and shorten the length size until the image appears.

Occasionally using the **undo button** will cause the preview screen to turn black; unfortunately the only thing to do is turn the machine off. Your work will be lost and you have to start again.

Cartridge Errors

Sometimes dust or debris accumulates in the cartridge port gently blow out any paper fiber that may have collected in the opening. Make sure the contact points are clean and that nothing is preventing the cartridge from being read properly.

With any electrical machine overheating can be a problem. If you get a cartridge error after using your machine for a while turn it off and let it cool down for about fifteen minutes.

If this is the very first time you're using the cartridge and you get an error I'm sure you know to try the trick about turning the cartridge around and inserting it in backward.

If you thought you could use your Imagine cartridges with your Expression 2, think again. You will get an error message because you can only use the **art cartridges** that you can cut with, the colors and patterns cartridge are for printing.

Even brand-new items fresh out of the box can be defective. If you see a cartridge error 1, 2, 3, 4, 5, 6, 9 or 99 call customer service and tell them the name, serial number and error message number and they may replace the cartridge.

Trouble Connecting to Your Computer

All Cricut machines come with a USB cord that lets you connect to your computer and allows you to use the other products like the Cricut Design Studio software, Cricut Craft Room or the Cricut Gypsy with your machines. (See the Warranty Warning chapter for update information on the DS and Gypsy.)

Double check your USB connection and try another port.

Check to see if you may have a firewall or anti-virus software that is blocking the connection.

See if you're running the latest firmware. You may need to update. Older machines update via firmware (Personal Cutter, Expression, Create and Cake) the newer (Expression 2, Imagine and Gypsy) use the Sync program to update.

When All Else Fails:

I know that no one wants to hear this. But there are going to be times when you may have to resort to calling customer service. This is especially true if your machine is still under warranty. You don't' want to do anything that might void the warranty on a machine that is truly defective.

Sadly, Prove Craft is known for its long wait times and sometimes less than stellar service. Stick it out and demand that your machine is fixed or replaced.

Chapter Two - Help With Cricut Cartridges

Tips for working with physical and digital cartridges, single images, sets and even bundle rentals too.

Cartridges are an ongoing discussion among Cricut users for a variety of reasons. We will discuss some of those issues in this chapter.

A cartridge is what contains the images and fonts that you'll be cutting. Most cartridges hold 700 or 800 images. Lite cartridges contain about 50 images and have one or two creative features. Despite the limitations you can still be creative and produce hundreds of variations with this less expensive choice.

You usually receive at least one cartridge with the purchase of your machine. Sometimes this is preloaded into your machine as a digital cartridge. You may buy downloadable digital cartridges online for immediate use or you can buy the physical plastic cartridges that you slide into your machine.

When you purchase a cartridge; you can use that physical cartridge in your machine or you also have the option to link that cartridge to the Cricut Craft Room (CCR).

The Craft Room allows you to view your images on your computer screen which makes it easier to see and manipulate your projects.

By linking to CCR, you won't have to bother to physically switch out your cartridges. If you plan to ever **sell the cartridges** then do NOT link them. Once they are linked you are not legally allowed to sell them. This is understandable. Some people might link them to the Craft Room so they have access to the images and then sell the physical cartridge.

The complaint that users have is that Provo Craft doesn't provide a way to unlink cartridges that you no longer want to use or keep. Hopefully, they will correct this sometime in the future.

To link your cartridges you'll need to do the following. Load the cartridge you want to add into your machine. Go online to the Craft Room. Under all cartridges select my cartridges. You will see a list of cartridges. Find the cartridge you want to add and click Link and follow the prompts.

Another advantage to adding your cartridges to the Craft Room is that you'll be able to pull images from several cartridges to use at one time. When you're using the physical cartridge you can only use images from one cartridge at a time.

If you buy a used cartridge you need to ask if it's linked. If it is, you will still be able to use the **physical cartridge in your machine but you will not be able to link it to the Craft Room.** A cartridge can only be linked once. It is possible to still use the cartridge in the Craft Room but you can't link it. You'll have to have the physical cartridge in your machine to cut the images.

It is now possible to purchase cartridges online and download them to your account. This means you don't have to wait for a physical cartridge to arrive in the mail. You have immediate access to the images. These are the digital cartridges that I referred to earlier.

Many people complain that the cartridges are too expensive. Instead of spending $80 on a cartridge with hundreds of images many people would prefer to be able to buy an image they really want for a dollar or two, that's where **single images or sets come in to play**.

You can buy single digital images or smaller sets for a fraction of the cost of a full cartridge. You can even rent cartridge bundles for 30 days on a **monthly subscription** on the Cricut home page under the shopping section.

Make sure you take advantage of the free cartridges offered in the Craft Room. The only thing to remember is to finish your projects. Once the cartridge is no longer free, you will not be able to cut your image.

You can save money on cartridges watching for sales and special promotions. We'll talk about ways to save money on cartridges in a later chapter.

It is possible to share physical cartridges with friends. This is good if they want a few images for a special project but don't plan to use the cartridge enough to justify buying it.

At one time you could use third party software to design your own images for use with the Cricut. But Provo Craft has currently made all their machines incompatible with third party software. Users were not happy with this turn of events, but so far Provo Craft has not backed down. You can manipulate the cartridge images in many ways to create unique designs. But the images must exist in a cartridge that you own to be able to cut them out.

Digital Handbooks for Easy Reference

Did you know you can download the digital handbook of any cartridge and save it as a PDF file on your computer? Just go to Cricut.com click on shop, images, and cartridges. Select any cartridge click on it scrolling down the page till you see the link for the digital handbook, open it and save it to your hard drive for easy reference.

Sharing Cut Files

A cut file is basically a project that someone has already created and laid out on their Cricut. They saved the file and shared it on their blog or in the Craft Room. What this does is it saves you from recreating the wheel so to speak.

If you see a project you like you can save the file onto your computer. Then go to the Craft Room and import that file. You can then make the same cuts without having to figure out how to lay everything out. The images are already sized and laid out for you.

The advantage of this is you can save yourself a lot of time by using layouts that others have already created.

But here's the tricky part, you must already own the cartridges the images are from. You can't make the cuts if you don't own the cartridges the images originated from.

You can also save your own projects and share them in the Craft Room for others to use.

When you see a cute project on Pinterest or on a craft blog, you might want to ask if the cut file is available and if so, what cartridges it uses.

Organization

If you're like most crafters, including me, you'll eventually become overrun with craft "stuff." You'll have paper stacks, vinyl rolls and other material that you're planning to use someday spread all over your craft area.

Your cartridges may be lying around in a pile and you have to spend twenty minutes searching every time you need a specific overlay or booklet.

Eventually, this creates such a feeling of chaos and frustration that you dread going into your craft room or crafting area.

This can all be solved with some organization. It may take you a few hours to get it all in order, but it will save you countless hours in the future. You'll no longer feel depressed every time you look at your crafting space.

Craft stores will often have storage containers specially made for certain types of crafts. But you may want to start at your local chain stores. They often have craft and office supply departments where you can find storage units cheaply.

You can find containers where you can sort all your paper into small shelves based on color and type of paper. If you don't like the ones at the craft store then try an office supply store. If you live in an area that's extremely humid; you may want to store your **paper in plastic containers**.

Another option is to watch for garage sales that say "craft items." Many people spend hundreds of dollars getting set up for a particular craft and then discover they don't have the time or inclination to spend much time actually doing the craft. This can be a bonanza for other crafters.

Photo boxes can be used to keep your booklets and overlays safe and organized.

Some crafters copy their overlays, **laminate them and bind them together** on rings where they can easily be added or removed.

There are special carrying cases, binders and totes designed just for cartridges. (For cheap Cricut products check out the resource chapter for online deals.)

Computer Files

Along with organizing your physical items; you might want to give some thought to organizing your computer files. It's always good to have a Cricut file to save all your cut files. But you'll eventually want to go a step further. You might want to organize your cut files by project type.

In other words; one for cards, one for scrapbook images, another for signs and one for quilt shapes.

The important thing is to give this some thought in the beginning. It's easier to set up a **computer file system** in the beginning.

Keeping everything organized at the start rather than to pile everything into one file and try to sort it all out later.

Travel Tips

You may occasionally want to travel with your Cricut to crafting events. It's good to have a sturdy case or tote to carry your die cutting machine that prevents it from shaking around too much. You also want to have room to bring a few supplies.

Resist the urge to bring everything! If you know what projects you'll be working on once you're there it will make it much easier to pack the right amount of paper or card stock that you'll need. Bring some extra in case of mistakes.

If you're able to connect to your laptop and work in the Craft Room then you won't need to bring all your physical cartridges. But you might want to bring a few in case the Wi-Fi connection is bad and for some reason you are not able to connect.

Remember; do not leave your Cricut in your car for extended periods of time if the temperature is extremely hot or cold. The machine should never be left in the direct sunlight.

Chapter Three - Ending the Blade Blues

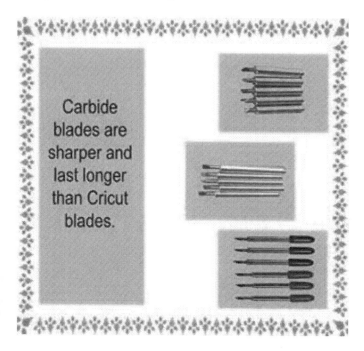

Carbide blades are sharper and last longer than Cricut blades.

Another one of the big problem areas I hear about is with the blades and the housing.

I know, as we've discussed before, we all want to take the machine out of the box and start popping parts on here and there where they look like they fit. We've all done it. Sometimes it even works.

Or sometimes we install things backward or not tight enough or too tight and end up causing ourselves a lot of unnecessary stress.

Take a few moments to read through the instruction manual. It will be painful, but it won't kill you. I'll be the first to admit that Cricut manuals aren't that great, they leave out a lot of details. However, in general you'll do better reading the instructions than ignoring them and just winging it.

Also, if you do have a problem you can't fix and need to use your warranty; you want to be sure you've followed directions and haven't done anything that would void your warranty.

For an extra safe tip always remember to unplug your machine or at the very least make sure it is turned off when installing or replacing the blade. These cutting blades are sharp and you do need to take common sense precautions. If you have small children make sure they can't access the machine when you're not around.

Installing the Blade

When you first get your machine; you'll need to install the blade housing. Your machine should be set on a stable table that won't shake and has at least two feet of space to load and unload your cutting mat.

Look through the box and make sure you received all the parts. This will include the blade and housing, your power cord to plug the machine in, the USB cord to connect to your computer, and all your manuals and quick start guide. (If you lose your manual you can do a search and find an online version in PDF form and save it on your computer.) You should also have some plastic dust covers that pop into your machine to …well…keep the dust out.

Open the front of your machine and take out any cardboard you see. This is placed in the machine to keep everything in place during shipping. You need to remove any cardboard or tape that will prevent the parts from moving.

Your blade should already be installed in the housing unit. To double check you will need to push the little button on the top to get the blade to pop out. If the plastic covering is still protecting the tip remove it.

You then need to unscrew the blade holder in the machine so it will swing out. Don't unscrew it so much that the nut completely comes off. Remember "righty tighty, lefty loosey." In other words, turn the knob to the left to loosen it. Install the blade housing with the arrow facing forward and the blade on the bottom. Then tighten the nut so the blade housing is secure. It shouldn't be wobbly or loose.

Watch out for this newbie mistake when installing your blade housing for the first time. Make sure the **arms fit around the first indentation and not the second one closest to the blade.** No matter how much you increase the blade depth, it will never cut in this position because the blade will never reach the paper.

The blade depth is actually located there on the blade housing (numbers 1 thru 6) as opposed to the other settings that are controlled by the screen and keyboard or by dials. You'll probably want to set the blade depth at 2 or 3 in the beginning. But you will need to adjust this if your cuts are not being made properly or when you use extremely thick material.

Changing the Blade

After a while you'll notice that your cuts are not as clean as they once were. Make sure there is no lint or adhesive glue sticking to the blade. If you have adjusted your settings to make sure the pressure and blade depth is correct for the material you are cutting and that the speed is correct for the size and type of image you selected and nothing has improved, it may be time to replace the blade.

It's estimated that each blade will last for 500 to 1,500 cuts. But that is determined by what material you're cutting. So it's very hard to estimate how long a blade can last.

You remove the blade housing by unscrewing the nut on the side of the housing until it swings out. Pull the housing out of the machine. Push the button on the housing and very carefully pull the blade out with tweezers or stick it into an old eraser and pull it out. Dispose of it carefully where it can't be picked up or stepped on accidentally.

The new blade will usually come with a plastic cover over the sharp edge. Be careful as you remove the plastic tip on the blade for obvious reasons. It's sharp! It's a good idea to place this plastic tip over the old blade before throwing it away.

Then slide the new blade into the housing. It is held in place by a magnet. The magnet will pull the blade into the housing with a snap and hold it in place. You won't need to push it in to get it to stay. You will hear it click when the magnet sucks up the blade.

Then put the housing back into the holder in the machine and screw the nut on the side until the housing is secure.

Deep Cut Blade

You'll want to use the deep cutting blade when cutting thicker material such as vinyl or chipboard. It comes with its own housing so you'll replace the entire housing, not just the blade.

Scoring Tip

You may have seen the suggestion that tells you to turn the blade around using the dull end to emboss or score with. I know a lot of people have tried this and liked it but let me tell you what happened to a friend of mine who tried it and wished she hadn't. Apparently, the bearings were scratched inside the housing and she had to replace it.

If you don't want to buy a scoring blade at least you have **been warned what may happen**.

Carbon Steel Blades

There's nothing more frustrating than buying replacement blades that are **dull right out of the package**. The lack of quality control has caused some Cricuter's to look for alternatives.

It seems there are a number of **compatible blades** on the market. These other brands make a 45° blade that is compatible with the Cricut regular blade and 60° blade that works like the Cricut deep cut blade. Here are some suggestions.

Gazelle Blades

Roland Blades

Clean Cut Blades

These carbon steel blades may be more expensive but they tend to be sharper and last longer. Just do a search for the brand name and the size you want like this 45° Roland cutting blade to find a variety of price points to choose from.

Cutting Problems

If you've adjusted all your settings and the material is still tearing then you may have to call the Provo Craft service desk to ask for help. There have been some machines sold that have defective housings. If you're unfortunate enough to get a defective machine then you want to be sure to return it to the company before your warranty has expired.

It's always a good idea to try your new machine on **several types of material within the first few weeks**. This way, if there's a problem you'll find it quickly.

Make sure you **save your receipt**! Provo Craft will not honor your warranty unless you have your receipt.

I've talked to some crafters who prefer to buy their machines through Amazon because they feel their return policy is better than buying directly from Provo Craft.

Chapter Four - Cutting Mat Miracles

Mats are a problem area for many Cricut users. They often feel like Goldilocks – this mat is too sticky and this mat is not sticky enough. Finding the "just right" mat can be tricky. In this chapter we will discuss some ways of caring for your mats and making them last as long as possible.

Cutting mats come in various sizes. The smaller ones are 12 x 6, 12 x 8.5 and 12 x 12. The largest one is 12 x 24. The mats have a sticky surface so they hold your paper in place while it is cut.

The mats were not designed to last for the life of your machine. You will need to replace them periodically. However, there are ways to extend the life of your mat which we'll be talking about in this chapter.

Be sure you press the paper down firmly on the mat. This is particularly useful if your mat has just started losing its stickiness. Make sure the paper is firmly stuck to the mat before loading the mat into the machine.

One way to extend the life of your mat is to switch back and forth occasionally from the **landscape to portrait mode**. This means your cuts will be spread more evenly over the mat. Otherwise the mat will soon start to show wear and tear from the same area being used the most.

I know the mats are supposed to be directional meaning you load it with the arrow pointing toward the machine, but I have known some to say they **alternate loading** the mat from the bottom to extend the life, so the same area is not always being cut.

One complaint I hear from Cricut users is their new mats are sometimes too sticky. This is a rather easy fix. Get a clean t-shirt or some other clean material and as lint free as possible and simply press it on the mat. It should remove the excess stickiness. Then use a lint roller over the mat. You can also use your hands and pat the mat, the oil from your hands will reduce the tackiness.

Matter of fact, I use a lint roller on my mat after every few cuts. A little lint stuck to the mat or to the blade can ruin your cut and rip the paper.

If your mat has lost its stickiness there are numerous ways to "restick" it. However, it is important to note that if your machine is under warranty that adding adhesive to the mat can void the warranty. So consider your options before deciding to do this, wait until your warranty has expired. Buying a new mat might be a better solution.

Some people use baby wipes to clean their mats or just simply wash the mat with soap and water. You can use your spatula to scrape any excess paper or gunk off your mat. If you don't have a spatula a credit or gift card will also work.

Cleaning and Resticking Your Mat

After a while your mat will have a variety of gunk stuck to it. One way to clean the mat is with a product called Goo Gone. The first thing you need to do is cover the edges of the mat with blue painter's tape. You don't want any cleaning or adhesive product to be on the part of the mat that goes **under the rollers in your machine**. This can cause your mat to not move through the machine cleanly and to get gunk on the rollers.

After all the edges are covered with tape; spray the mat with the product. Three or four sprays are sufficient. You don't want to overspray. Then let the mat sit for ten or fifteen minutes.

Then take a small nail brush, a toothbrush will even work, and scrub the mat carefully. The stuff should come off easily. If not, you can spray it again and let the mat sit longer. But most paper remnants and glitter will start to come off. Then get a clean rag and just wipe the mat off.

Next, you'll need a product called Easy Tac. Spray the mat lightly. Again, you don't want to over spray. Follow the directions and only use this product in a well-ventilated area. Let the mat sit for at least fifteen minutes before you use it again. You don't want it to be wet when it goes through your machine. It's not a bad idea to let it sit overnight before using it again. Don't forget to remove the tape from the edges when you're done!

Another product that some users have suggested to restick their mats is Alene's Tack-it Glues. With this product you'll need to have a foam brush or sponge and apply a thin layer of the glue to your mat. Add water to the glue in equal parts of glue and water before brushing it on.

Again, be sure it is completely dry before you try to use your mat. It is still important to cover the edges of your mat with tape before you apply any type of glue or adhesive.

I prefer the Easy Tac, myself. But you can try different products and see which works best for you.

Zig Two-Way Glue is another option. Because it comes out blue; you can be sure you're covering the entire mat since you can see clearly where you've applied the glue.

Another option some Cricuter's use is scotch taping their paper to their mat. They tape their paper on all four sides before loading the mat into their machine. Some use regular tape and others use double sided tape or painters tape. If this works for you it can save you from having to restick your mats.

If you don't have time to restick the entire mat and wait for it to dry then apply repositionable glue to the back of the card stock or chipboard you're working on for a quick fix.

Save some of your mats that have lost their sticking power because they still work well enough with gel pens or markers when all you want to do is draw.

Remember; when you're using any adhesive product on your mat let it completely dry before you try running the mat through the machine. Avoid getting adhesive on the sides of the mat where it can get onto the rollers.

Here's a real time-saving tip. Have several mats handy with the whole project laid out; now you can cut out all your designs at once.

Problems Loading The Mat

If you have trouble loading the mat into your machine I find that just unloading and reloading sometimes helps. Make sure you are loading the mat with the arrows pointing the right direction. However, I know some crafters who have had luck with loading the mat from a different direction, not the way the arrow was pointing and corrected the problem that way. So try it from a different direction and see if that helps.

Sometimes a slight **push down and forward**, giving it a gentle nudge will help the mat load.

Make sure the mat is under the plastic guides and not too far to the left or the right. It needs to go into the machine **completely straight**.

Have you ever tried loading the mat and all it does is vibrate against the rollers or you see the rollers moving, but they don't grab the mat? Try **reducing the pressure** for a simple fix.

Also, make sure the mat is not curled in any way. This can sometimes happen when the mat is shipped to you. Try a new mat and see if you still have the same problem.

The life of your mat is affected by how many cuts you make and how deep. Once the mat has enough cuts to make it rough feeling you may start having trouble with your paper tearing. In that case, it's time to replace the mat or make a new one! (See the video tutorial on making your own mats.)

Make sure all your images are in the **cut zone**. The Cricut does not cut the full size of the mat. (Unless you know this paper saving tip found in the video tutorial section.) There is a no-cut zone around the edges; it can cause a problem if your images are running over into that border area.

One final tip for all you frugal folks out there, here's how to get two for the price of one. Have you ever considered cutting a larger mat to make two smaller ones? One 12 x 24 mat suddenly becomes two 12 x 12 mats and a 12 x 12 mat yields two 6 x 12 mats.

Chapter Five - Working With Gel Pens and Markers

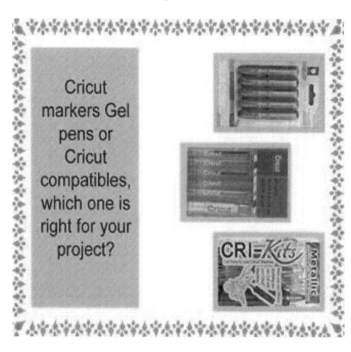

Cricut markers Gel pens or Cricut compatibles, which one is right for your project?

Another great option you have with your Cricut machine is using markers to create images as opposed to cutting the images out. This gives you a multitude of choices for card making. I like to use the markers to outline before I make cuts. This makes the cut images stand out more. It's just another creative way to use your Cricut.

The pens can also add designs within the cuts. For example, a Mickey Mouse image might cut out the shape of Mickey, but the pen will draw the details inside the shape such as his eyes and clothing.

With this design option you can turn any image into custom stickers or make coloring books with all your kid's favorite characters.

Pens are also good for shading or highlighting cuts.

You'll have to remove the blade housing and replace it with a marker or a pen holder. I always put a piece of scrap paper under the pen so I don't write on my mat or paper accidentally.

You can NOT move the carriage at all when you switch out the pen and blade. If you do, **then the cut and the outline the pen made will not match**. To match exactly you need to be sure you don't move the carriage at all.

Select the image you want to draw and hit the cut button; the marker will draw the design. If you want to cut it out, press the load paper button and the carriage will return to the starting point. Never unload the mat because your images will not line up. Remove the marker and install the blade housing. (I know I told you to always turn off your machine when working with the blade, but this is the exception. If you turn off the machine it will forget the last instruction, so **don't turn it off, just be careful.**) Now press the repeat last key and the cut button and watch the magic happen.

You can purchase markers and gel pens from Provo Craft. There are also other compatible pens and markers from other manufacturers. For the best quality look for pens that are acid-free, **archival safe, do not bleed or fade and are waterproof.**

Follow the settings given on the maker. You may have to increase the pressure and speed when you are done drawing and want to cut out the image.

Markers will usually provide a darker, wider line. Gel pens are better for thinner, lighter lines. Which to use will depend on the end result you desire for your project.

You can also lower the pressure to obtain thinner lines. The harder the pen is pressing down the darker and wider the line will be. But don't increase the pressure too much or it will ruin the tip of the pen.

Not only can you find a variety of different colors; there are also metallic colors such as bronze, gold and silver. These can add an entirely different look to cards. You can also get glitter pens too.

Another use for the markers is to use them to **preview** how a cut will look on vinyl. This can help you choose the best font or size for your project and avoid wasting vinyl. Just try different options with the pens until you find the one you like best. Then make your cuts.

Chapter Six - Used Cricuts the Good the Bad and the Ugly

A popular way to save money on Cricut machines is to buy them used. That can be an especially good idea if you're in a crafting club or group and know who you're buying from. Crafters often want to upgrade and will sell their old machines cheaply.

Also, we know there are always people who go "gung-ho" into a hobby and buy everything available. A few months later they're bored and want to move on to something else. One of the big advantages of buying a used machine is that you may also get extra supplies or cartridges.

You can sometimes find used machines on eBay and Amazon. The obvious downside to this is you have no way of knowing if the machine works or at least works well. It can be a hassle to try and get your money back. If the seller has a rating it can give you some idea if they are reputable in their dealings.

Another option is Craigslist. This does have the advantage of being a local seller. You can visit the seller and see how the machine works before you buy.

When purchasing a used machine ask to see it cut several types of material. A machine that works great on paper might have problems cutting card stock. You might want to bring some material with you in case the seller doesn't have card stock or vinyl so you can do test cuts yourself.

If you're buying cartridges with the machine you should always **ask if the cartridges have been linked**. If they have then you'll only be able to use the cartridges when you have them physically loaded into your machine, they will still cut but you won't be able to relink them in the Craft Room or the Gypsy.

Ask the seller if they bought the machine new and how long they've had it. Also, ask why they're selling. Many times it's just because they decided they don't have time for crafting or don't enjoy scrapbooking as much as they thought they would. But it could be they're having a lot of problems with the machine. Of course, they won't often admit this to you. But sometimes you can tell a lot simply by their hesitation when you ask the question.

Garage sales and thrift stores are another possible way to find used machines. Again, the advantage is they often come with several cartridges included and you get to **test the machine** to see if it is still working properly.

Buying a used machine can be a great bargain, but as the saying goes, "buyer beware." Try to get as much information as you can before you make your purchase. Ask about customer satisfaction and if there is a money back guarantee.

Having the right supplies makes your job easier. Use acid netural and archival safe products for good results.

A big question with new scrapbookers and crafters is; what is the best adhesive to use.

I admit to being personally fond of glue dots. You can find them online and in most craft stores. They're a permanent adhesive and maintain their bond on many types of material. They're easy to use and I don't worry about getting too much glue squeezed out of a bottle accidentally. They're also less messy than many other kinds of glue and can be used for small pieces of projects. Pop-up dots add dimension to any project, they just peel and stick to everything from paper to wood, fabric, plastic and even metal.

Many crafters swear by their double-sided adhesive tape applied with a gun or glider. The Scotch Applicator Gun is one of the best choices. It uses an acid neutral tape that will not damage family photos or yellow any paper. The Scotch ATG applicator can hold a roll of 1/4 inch or 1/2 inch tape, just right for most Cricut crafts.

The applicator releases the tape in an accurate and easy to use manner. It removes and stores the liner as it releases the tape. The roll of tape is very large and lasts a long time. I find this to be well worth the money and usually look for deals on several rolls of refill tape and stock up. There are cheaper versions but I haven't found one that works as well.

For acid-free and archival safe glue, the Zig family of glue pens is a popular choice. The fine tip pen is perfect for applying glue to your intricate designs. Or you can use the wide mouth roller for bigger jobs. Depending on how you apply it, this glue is permanent or repositionable.

Zip Dry Paper Glue is not just for paper but also works with all kinds of embellishments like glitter, beads and metal. What's really nice is it doesn't leave any sticky residue on your finger when you wipe it off, if you make a mistake or change your mind.

Xyron adhesives seem to be popular with crafters and come in a whole line of products; their sticker maker is on my wish list.

I enjoy the American Crafts card stock. The color goes all the way through which means you don't end up with the white core on layered projects.

Some card stocks I've tried are simply too fibrous and don't cut well and often leave a big mess behind.

When trying to cut thin paper it's often a good idea to tape around the edges. This seems to keep it from slipping. Personally, I find really thin paper some of the hardest to cut without tearing.

I have also had good luck the Bazzil and Recollections brands. They can be found at most craft stores or online.

If you're looking for designer paper with more options you may want to try K and Company Designer, but they are a bit pricey.

Remember if you're cutting thicker card stock you may need to use the **multi cut function**. This means the cutting blade will go over the cut up to four times to make sure it's cutting all the way through.

I have a teacher friend who has tried to use the cheap construction paper she's supplied with at her school. It usually rips and sticks badly to the mat. Slowing the speed down and using an old mat helps some.

One type of paper I've heard many complaints about is the single sheet paper and card stock at Hobby Lobby. Many users seem to have a problem with this brand.

Card stock: I personally find 65 lb. card stock to work the best. Thinner stock doesn't handle intricate cuts as well and thicker wears out my blades too quickly.

Adhesive backed craft vinyl is another material I like to use. It's more expensive than buying regular vinyl but it's easier to use since the adhesive is already added. It usually provides a smoother surface than risking lumps of glue when you attach the vinyl.

When working with vinyl some prefer the KISS Cut method where you just cut thru the vinyl leaving the backing intact, rather than cutting all the way thru.

Accessories You Might Want to Add

When I first purchased my machine I also added the Cricut Tool Kit. I have to say I've never regretted this purchase. It contains seven tools and I use them all. The seven pieces include a small pair of scissors which I use on intricate designs, a craft knife that is perfect for removing projects from the mat, a hook tool great for vinyl, a scoop, a bone folder for scoring paper, a ruler and a scarper. They come in a plastic bag for easy storage.

I've recently added a very sharp pair of needle nose scissors and a few old dental picks to my arsenal. I just lift and snip anything that doesn't cut all the way, works like a charm. (My hook tool broke and rather than buying another kit I just asked my dentist to save any picks he was discarding, free is always good.)

Another tool I use a lot is the spatula. I find this to be the most practical for removing projects from the mat without tearing them.

I keep a lint roller to roll across the mat to pick up small pieces of fiber that stick to the mat.

Tweezers come in handy for just about everything.

I always keep at least one deep cut blade on hand for when I'm cutting thicker card stock. This keeps me from wearing out my regular blade as quickly.

It's never a bad idea to have extra mats on hand. If you don't have time to restick your mat and have a late night project to finish; having that extra mat can save a lot of stress.

Blue painters tape is always a good supply for any craft room. It can be used to cover mats if you spray them with adhesive. It can also be used to hold paper to a mat if the mat has lost all of it stickiness.

Provo Craft comes up with new products from time to time but before I buy anything, I like to wait until I've heard a few comments from friends or read reviews in Cricut forums before I purchase. It's always good to know if others had good luck with the product before spending money on it.

Chapter Eight - Money Saving Tricks

For money savings bargains search for Cricut lot or lots on eBay.

We've already talked about saving money by buying a used Cricut. It can be a great way to get a machine at a drastically reduced price. It might work out fine or it might not. There are always risks with used machines. Refer back to Chapter Six for the best places and ways to buy used machines.

When you first buy your machine; you may be offered a special package deal to purchase tools or cartridges at a reduced rate. This can often be a good way to take advantage of discount pricing. Search for **Cricut bundle or bundles** when looking for deals.

Another way to save money is by watching for sales at your local hobby stores. If you get on their email list you can often get coupons for 10% - 25% off sales.

Watch for sales online and offline. Hobby stores will often run sales on paper and other materials. Even the Cricut cartridges often go on sale. So always look at the flyers or emails they send you.

If you find a particular brand or type of paper you might want to consider buying in bulk.

A lot of crafting clubs have email lists and share information about the latest sales at hobby stores and online.

Another option is to buy bulk packages with your crafting group and then divide them.

I know some crafters get vinyl from sign shops. They can buy pieces at much lower rates. Some sign shops even give them their scraps for free.

As we talked about in the cartridge chapter; you can save money by sharing or borrowing cartridges from friends.

Garage sales are another way to possibly save money. A friend of mine recently found a Cricut machine at a garage sale for a hundred dollars, doesn't seem like a great deal until you consider it came with ten cartridges.

Sign up for the Cricut Rewards program. When you buy products you'll get points that you can then use to buy other products when they are in stock. All the good deals seem to go fast though!

My Favorite Bargain Hunting Tips:

We all know that craft supplies bought at specialty stores can be expensive. Often times you can get the exact same item or a similar substitute at considerable savings if you think like a **bargain hunter rather than a crafter**. So the next time you're shopping for craft supplies consider these venues and enjoy the savings.

My personal favorite is the good old .99 cents store

Clearance, wholesale and discontinued merchandise type stores

Thrift stores and junk shops

Home improvement and hardware stores, office supply stores

Yard sales, flea markets or car boot sales

Charity auctions, rummage sales and bazaars

Reverse auction, penny auctions and white elephant sales

Pennysaver want ads, community bulletin boards and online classified ads

Remember one man's or woman's trash is another's treasure. Often time's people don't know the value of their unwanted or unused items, but you do! And if by chance you run across a super bargain, scoop it up, if you can't find a use for it, you can always sell it or trade it.

Tell your family and friends to keep an eye out for craft supplies when they shop and to have your phone number handy when they find a bargain.

Consider **group buys**. Even higher-priced items can be within your reach if you share the cost with friends. When you pool your resources with other crafters you get more for your money.

Trade or barter. If a friend has an item you'd love to own but you have nothing to trade, think outside the box. Provide a useful service like babysitting, running errands, doing yard work or make a fantastic dessert. Being helpful will do wonders for your friendship not to mention winning you the coveted prize.

Wholesale and lot buys. When looking for **deals on eBay** make sure to include the words wholesale, lots or lot in your keyword search.

If you are looking for Cricut lots, here is a good place to start. http://cricutdiecuttingmachine.com/Store/cricut-lots

You can also search by specific category to find wholesale lots. http://www.ebay.com/sch/allcategories/all-categories

Look at the bottom of each category and you should see wholesale lots, if not click on see more and look for it. When you find the wholesale lots link click on it and you'll be taken to the search page. Use broad terms like crafts, scrapbooking, rubber stamps to get the most results. I did a search in the collectibles category clicked on **wholesale lots** and typed in the keyword **junk drawer** and found a ton of cool embellishments.

Or just type in junk drawer jewelry from the **eBay home page** and sort by lowest price to find all the beads you could ever want to decorate anything on the cheap.

Reuse, repurpose and recycle. The .99 cents store is filled with craft supplies **that didn't start out as such**. It's stocked with plastic storage containers that with a little imagination can be turned into cartridge storage totes.

Here's a helpful hint. Have in mind the storage container you're trying to copy. Search online or visit your craft store and take note of the dimensions and the style. That way when you're at the .99 cents store you will know what to look for and how much modification you will have to make to duplicate the expensive storage tote.

Make your own storage pockets for cartridge overlays and booklets that fit into binders by looking for clear plastic sleeves.

Hardware stores carry trays with little compartments for storing nuts and bolts. Look for ones that will hold your cartridges.

Some toolboxes come with inserts or trays that are partitioned off into little compartments. Check to see if the dimensions are the right size for your cartridges. A word to the wise, make sure your hubby has no further use for his toolbox trays BEFORE you grab them. This might be an item you look for at flea markets or yard sales rather than his workshop or garage.

Old fishing tackle boxes are also a source of trays and inserts that may just be the right size. If they don't fit your cartridges consider using them for other embellishments like beads, tags, rhinestones, buttons or charms.

Cropping parties are a great way for like-minded people to meet and have fun. You can share your product recommendations as well as your favorite tips and tricks. Why not suggest or organize a **swap meet** at your next crop. Bring your supplies or completed projects that you are willing to trade or swap with other crafters.

Let's say you love making greeting cards or you went wild and created a bunch of scrapbooking layouts and another party goer has brought a bunch of stickers she'd like to trade for your completed scrapbook pages; you get the idea.

Chapter Nine - Conquering Craft Room Chaos

Clutter and chaos rob you of your crafting time. Keep your craft space organized with these time saving tips.

There's nothing worse than spending your precious crafting time hunting for supplies, rather than creating beautiful projects. Here are some helpful organizational hints that will keep everything in its place and make it super easy to find.

When space is limited consider using every available surface for storage, like the back of a door, the edge of a shelf, the space under a cabinet above the counter and if you're really desperate for space install an overhead storage system on the ceiling.

If you don't have a craft room but use the kitchen table instead here are some smart suggestions. Keep all your supplies neatly organized in a **suitcase on wheels**. That way you can easily move and store everything you need in one place.

How about turning a rolling kitchen island into a **portable craft room**? The butcher block or stainless steel tops provide an excellent work surface, and the drawers or shelves furnish needed storage.

Is the Craftbox on your wish list? This is specialized furniture for crafters that cost about 900 bucks. But I like my money-saving suggestions better. Can you convert a closet into a craft room? What about a **used armoire, bookshelf or an old entertainment center**, with the addition of a drop-down table all you need is a chair.

Don't throw away those baby food jars; they make great **storage containers**. To conserve counter space, you might try nailing or screwing the lids of the jars onto a board and then attach the board under your cabinets above the counter. Then simply fill the jars and screw them into the lids. All those tiny hard-to-find items will be displayed nicely in the row of jars.

Turntables are not just for records. Use Lazy Susan's to organize items you use routinely instead of throwing them in a drawer. You can build stackable rotating trays and triple your available storage. Tin cans or mason jars fit nicely on the round trays and hold any number of items.

No wasted real estate here. Remember I mentioned the back of the door well this is the perfect place to hang a **see-through plastic shoe organizer**. It comes with dozens of pockets that are perfect to stuff full of craft supplies. Do a search on the Internet for door pockets or over the door organizer to find dozens of styles to choose from. If you like to sew you can make your own out of fabric. You can organize the items alphabetically or by category or by how often used. Make sure to label each pocket for easy identification.

You can mount a magnetic tool strip or self-adhesive magnetic tape to the edge of a shelf or counter. Any metal tool that you use often will be right at your fingertips.

Another **under the counter trick** is to install a wooden closet dowel, that's the rod your clothes hang on. Then attach clear plastic pockets to close hangers and fill them up.

Pegboards can be configured in 100 different ways. Customize yours horizontally and vertically to squeeze out every last inch of usable storage space.

String and embroidery floss can be kept from unraveling by wrapping them around clothespins and securing the end.

Any container with a plastic lid like a coffee can or cottage cheese container is a cheap way to keep your yarn and ribbon organized. Just cut a hole in the plastic lid and thread the yarn or ribbon through it pulling out as much as you need each time.

Try to keep rolls of vinyl on hangers or somewhere they can remain rolled up instead of getting squished by having something set on them. This can crinkle the vinyl and increase the odds of it tearing as it goes through the machine.

Templates save time. If you have favorite greeting card designs and scrapbook layouts that you reuse consider making templates. Create your favorite templates and keep them in a binder or punch a hole in them and keep them on a ring. That way you can flip through them and never be stuck for an idea.

My friend Katina is the most organized crafter in the world. Visit her blog to learn a bunch of great tips and tricks. Her mission is to

inspire and help you with all your paper craft projects.
http://www.lovinglifeslittleblessings.com/

Bring a smile to someone's face and make their day special with a personalized greeting card just for them!

I'll never forget the look on my husband's face when he met the postman and thumbed through the mail expecting the usual ads and of course a bill or two. Then suddenly he came across an envelope with his name on it, written in my handwriting. A puzzled look on his face gave way to a big grin as he read the handcrafted card filled with heartfelt sentiment. That beautiful smile filled his face, and a tear welled up in his eye.

My husband is an avid sailor, but the pressures of life and the unexpected demands on his time kept him from enjoying the ocean blue for quite some time.

So I created a card chock full of sailing motifs and filled it with loving sentiment and mailed it to him. Needless to say we spent the next three Saturdays on the old Catamaran out on the ocean enjoying each other's company.

So ladies when designing your card make it as personal as possible by using a theme that's near and dear to his heart for lasting memories he will cherish.

Besides expressing your love why not invite him out for a night on the town and you'll pick up the check. Or tell him to expect the best home-cooked meal he has ever had. If you've had a bit of an argument, this is the perfect way of saying you're sorry and telling him you've planned a very special evening at home to make it up to him.

If you mail it to your home make sure he picks up the mail or if you send it to his office, write "personal to be opened by addressee only" so his secretary will not open it. Have fun with this tip, we certainly did.

Now if you have children create a custom card just for them. Fill it with praise, appreciation and recognition. Kids love getting mail addressed to them. They don't have to win the Nobel Prize for you to commend them. Any simple event will do. Thank them for their help around the house, doing better at school, or if discipline was administered tell them you have confidence in them that they won't repeat the offense. Make sure to tell them about the special day you have planned especially for them. Why not give this tip a try too.

One final thought I never knew how much my mother valued the cards I sent her till she died. I found a stack of cards I sent her over the years; she kept every one. Had I known that, I would've sent her many more. So friends get busy making those cards.

Chapter Eleven - Warranty Warning

Provo Craft has decided to discontinue the Cricut Imagine, Cake and Create machines, as well as the Gypsy and the Design Studio software. The Gypsy and Design Studio have not been updated since April of 2013. Repair services are still offered on the Gypsy.

These discontinued machines can still be purchased from retailers while supplies last. Technical support will still be provided and the one-year warranty will be honored on registered machines.

Since these machines have been discontinued, knowing that may influence your buying decision, as support may vanish at any time.

Since the Cricut Cake machine has been discontinued some of you may decide to cut edible material with another machine. Please take note you'll **void the warranty** if you cut any material the machine was not designed to cut. Not to mention the cross-contamination meaning you'll have paper fibers in your frosting sheets and gum paste on your card stock.

Any do it yourself repairs should only be attempted on machines with expired warranties.

For Cheat sheets, gigantic cutting guide and the best Cricut deals online vist these handy dandy resources.

The number one reason you have to buy a new Cricut machine is when it stops cutting. Well let's see if we can change that with these Cricut hacks! Below you will find common cutting problems and some **do it yourself repair techniques**. Remember only try these repairs once your machine is out of warranty.

If the blade housing is not going up and down like it should the simplest repair is to check to see if anything has jammed it and clear out any debris. The next step is to remove the plastic housing and give the coils a little squirt of WD-40. Make sure to wipe off any excess that may dip off and reassemble the plastic cover.

The next simple fix when the blade housing is binding, drags across the paper or cuts thru your images is to **remove the cover and examine the leaf springs to see if they are bent out of shape**. Check the upper and lower springs to make sure they are even and flat not bent or twisted to one side. Give them a pinch to straighten them out.

This next repair involves the wiring. Remove the plastic cover on the carriage car and check to see if any of the red, yellow or black wires connected to the solenoid **have come loose and need to be screwed down again**. These tiny wires are delicate and the connections can easily come apart. You may also have to **replace any broken wires and resolder them** using a soldering gun. For complete step by step repair instructions see the video tutorial chapter.

Rebooting Your Machine

It seems the stock answer from customer support is do a hard reset when anything goes wrong with your machine, so I have included the instructions here.

Make sure the machine is on with no cartridge loaded. Turn all three dials down to the lowest settings. Gently move the blade assembly all the way to the left by pulling on the carriage. Look inside the machine in the back for a red button; hold it down for a good five seconds. Now roll the dials up and down several times. Finally press the cut button then turn the Cricut off and let it rest for twenty minutes which should clear the memory and restore the functionality of the die cutter.

For Expression users check out http://help.cricut.com/help/cricut-machine-screen-problems#expression2.

Look What You Can Cut	Blade	Pressure	Speed	Multi-Cut
Cardstock	5	5	2	1
Chipboard	*6	5	3	2
Contact Paper	3	3	3	NA
Fabric	6	5	4	1
Heavy Cardstock	*6	5	2	2
Magnet	*6	3	5	4
Stamp	*4	4	3	1
Stencil	6	5	3	2
Thin Plastic	6	5	4	NA
Transparency	3	4	3	NA
Vellum	4	3	3	NA
Vinyl	*4	3	4	1

* Indicates using a deep cut blade

For a gigantic cutting guide filled with over 500 settings for different kinds of material you can cut with your Cricut machine, visit my friend Megan at http://www.aboverubiesstudio.com/the-cricut-cutting-guide/

Have you seen the Cricut Whispers? These cheat sheets are a handy resource you keep right at your fingertips. Just flip thru the pages to find the answers to common Cricut problems. http://caramiller.com/if-i-made-the-whispers-whispers-to-go-would-that-make-it-easier-for-you/

Shop and save on cheap Cricut supplies, always in stock and ready to ship. http://cricutdiecuttingmachine.com

Chapter Thirteen - How to Video Tutorials

Cricut Markers

Michelle shows you how easy it is to use the Cricut markers to outline your image before cutting it.

https://youtu.be/wAfaCxHHEG4

Cricut Mats

The first part of the video shows you how to re-stick your mat, but in the last part she explains how to make your own Cricut mats out of cheap table placemats.

https://youtu.be/tTajr-dCebM

Cutting Fabric

I like this video because it teaches you two ways to cut fabric so you can see which one you like best.

https://youtu.be/jeblAO4aKbw

Saving Paper

This guy takes paper saving to a whole new level. You will learn how to squeeze in more shapes and make every cut count.

https://youtu.be/XAxU9RcfhA0

Favorite Products

Mel recommends some products she uses with her Cricut machine.

https://youtu.be/85muL-dloIs

How to Repair Your Cricut Machine

Has your machine stopped cutting? If your warranty has expired you have two choices, you can either buy a new machine or fix the one you have. Watch and see how easy it is to fix one of the most common problems Cricut machines have.

https://youtu.be/n7LJnfPd

Cheap Vinyl

Have you seen Cricut vinyl at the .99 centscar boot store? Look in the kitchen aisle for roles of shelf liner or contact paper. This is not re-positional vinyl that you would use for wall art. It's just a cheap alternative to have fun with.

https://youtu.be/vEKwwjryGQY

Cricut Craft Room for Beginners

I chose this video because she shares her fears about being new to the Cricut machine and having to learn even more using the software, so all you newbies take heart, if she can do it, you can too.

https://youtu.be/8eI6qk9Iy38

Engraving Metal with the Cricut

Here is how to engrave on thin metal with your cutter. Bosskut the makers of the Gazelle die cutter makes an engraving blade compatible with Cricut machines.

https://youtu.be/nxM_epJW80w

Nail Art

Create beautiful nails with this technique. Have you considered using your Cricut machine to cut vinyl images for fantastic nail art? Since nail polish comes in and endless variety of colors you can mix and match it with vinyl to come up with stunning designs. There are a ton of nail art videos to watch on YouTube and get ideas from. You're only limited by your imagination, so have fun with this tip.

Chapter Fourteen - FAQs

Here are some of the most frequently asked question and answers among Cricut users:

1. Is there any software I can use that will allow me to use my own designs? Currently no 3rd party software is compatible with older Cricuts. This wasn't always the case in the past and has made some unhappy Cricut users.

You can still manipulate designs by welding, kerning, flipping, rotating, grouping and shadowing your images. Visit YouTube and watch the helpful tutorials other crafters have posted to learn even more.

2. What types of material will a Cricut cut? Your Cricut will cut paper of various thicknesses. It will also cut card stock, vinyl, cardboard and cloth. But for each material you will need to adjust your settings. You may need to use the multi cut function for thicker material. Also, it's a good idea to switch to your deep cut blade for thicker material. (For a quick cutting chart and to learn what other stuff you can cut with your machine see the resource chapter.)

3. What is a Crop? This is just a get together for Cricut users and scrapbookers to share ideas and have fun.

4. Can I cut fabric with my Cricut? You can, but it does require some preparation. The best way is to stiffen the material someway so it doesn't slip or slide while it's being cut. You may also need to tape or add extra glue to also assure the material doesn't move. It's best to only cut simple images; not intricate cuts. You'll need to clean your mat and blade carefully after cutting fabric. You'll want to try several ways to stiffen the material and see which one works best for you. Heat n Bond fusible webbing works well.

5. Does is cost to join the Craft Room? No, this is provided by the Provo Craft company and there is no cost to join.

How can I learn how to use the Craft Room? The CCR has provided many video tutorials to help get you started. You can find them here:

https://youtu.be/TLcCBOwE2E?list=PLPvqhFCBvwhsj5G1w-6iHEeZyFAxawJbk

6. Where can I go to get help with my Cricut? Your first option is the customer service desk at Provo Craft. You can email them or call them. You are usually more likely to get help with a phone call. But the hold times can be long and some customer service representatives are more knowledgeable and helpful than others. Monday - Friday 9 a.m. - 8 p.m. (ET)

Toll free support: 877-727-4288 UK: 0808 101 7032 Intl.: 0044 0808 101 7032 email: support@cricut.com Live chat at https://help.cricut.com/

You can find lots of information in this forum as well as ask your own questions. There is even a sub-forum for teachers who use the Cricut for educational purposes. http://www.Cricut.com/forum unfortunately this forum has been retired. You can find additional information at https://www.facebook.com/OfficialCricut/ Get questions answered my sending a message.

There are also other forums for Cricut users that you can find by typing Cricut forums in your search engine.

Many blogs are dedicated to helping crafters in many areas; including Cricut information. Just type Cricut blogs into your search engine and see what you can find.

Forums come and go thank goodness there are also Facebook and Yahoo groups dedicated to Cricut users. You can also find many Pinterest pages that show off different project ideas.

7. What is a Gypsy? The Gypsy is a portable handheld design studio that works with your Cricut. It would be out of the scope of this book to explain the benefits of working with the Gypsy. I may tackle that in my next book.

8. I'm having trouble using the Craft Room with my Mac? Sadly, you're not alone. Provo Craft has supposedly worked out the issue regarding the security settings. It seems to happen most if Mac users have updated to Maverick on their Mac.

9. Can I have more than one computer authorized on my Craft Room account? Many people like to have their desktop and their laptop authorized for use in the Craft Room. This shouldn't be a problem since the Craft Room claims they allow two computers for each account. However, many users complain that they have to call customer service and unauthorize a computer every time they switch. This should not be the case; but apparently it is, at least for some users.

10. Is there an alternative to the Craft Room? Yes, to use a computer with one of the older Cricut machines you could try the Cricut Design Studio software on CD. It's still being sold on eBay and Amazon. The only drawback is it's compatible with older versions of Windows and may or may not work with newer versions.

11. What types of projects can you create with a Cricut machine? The sky is the limit. Many people, like me, originally bought it for scrapbooking projects. We wanted to be able to cut out a multitude of shapes and designs.

But after owning the machine for a while I began to play around with many other creative projects. I'm only going to mention a few to get your own creative juices flowing.

Besides scrapbooking, I think making your own **greetings cards** has got to be one of the most popular things to create. I love doing layered cards.

I haven't tried my hand at designing and cutting out my own **rubber stamps**, but I know others who have saved a bunch of money with this option.

You can also use designs from your Cricut to make **stencils** for t-shirts. There is even iron on heat transfer vinyl for clothes and home decor items like pillows and placemats. Or make your own appliques and apply them to fabric.

I've attached vinyl letters to canister sets, stemware, picture frames, mirrors and a wide variety of kid's toys. You can purchase old children's furniture at flea markets or garage sales and give them new life by painting them and then attaching cute vinyl designs.

Adorable **paper dolls** with a wide assortment of clothes can be made with the Cricut. These are a great low-cost gift idea.

Doll clothes can even be made if you know how to cut fabric. Cutting fabric isn't the easiest thing to do on the Cricut but with a little practice and patience you'll be a tailor in no time. Remember to stiffen the fabric so it runs through the machine properly.

Speaking of fabric; quilters have recently fallen in love with the Cricut. They can cut many **quilting shapes** with the Cricut in a short amount of time. These can then be sewn together to make amazing quilt patterns.

Magnets are another fun project. You'll probably need your deep cut blade to cut magnet material. You can even create your own refrigerator magnets for your club or business. Or just for fun and profit.

Glass etching and engraving metal is also possible using designs from your Cricut.

Though most people use their cutters for their own personal projects some users have created their own business **selling crafts** they make with their machine.

You can set up a booth at a craft fair or swap meet and personalize objects right there while customers wait.

Another option is to set-up your own website to sell your crafts. If you don't want the hassle of your own site Etsy.com or eBay is a great place to sell craft items without having to create your own website.

Just a closing thought

If I can make it a little easier for you to have fun with your die cut machine that would really make my day.

I had fun writing this Cricut Tips book for older machines and I feel it's a helpful, time-saving guide for Cricut users.

If you 've upgraded to any of the Explore machines and want help understanding how Design Space works then look for my Cricut Explore book. It's a step by step manual for Explore users.

Looking for home decorating ideas using craft vinyl? Then check out my Craft Vinyl Decorating Ideas book next.

Introduction to Craft Vinyl

If you own a die cut machine you know one of the most popular things to cut is craft vinyl. It's pretty easy to work with its loads of fun, and it sticks to almost any surface like walls, glass, metal, wood, stone, cloth, and most plastics.

As with any other material I've used with my Cricut machine; there was a learning curve. I had ruined a few projects before I figured it out. The reason I wrote this book was to save you some of the stress that I went through.

For newbies, this guidebook will provide the confidence and incentive you need to give vinyl a try. For all you experienced in the art of vinyl cutting, I hope this book will open your eyes to the endless possibilities decorating with craft vinyl provides.

Whether you're looking for home decorating tips, handmade gift ideas or you want to turn your love of crafting into a home-based business that pays for your supplies and puts a little cash in your wallet I'm here to help.

By the time you're finished reading this book, you should have the knowledge to enjoy doing vinyl projects with your die cutter -- minus the stress.

If you want the ultimate troubleshooting guide to help you master your Cricut machine check out my first Cricut Tips book.

This is going to be fun; so let's get started!

Chapter Fifteen - Vinyl Basics

In this chapter we're going to cover the basics of working with vinyl using your Cricut machine.

With the mass production of plastic in the 1940s, it seems to have permeated our lives. We use it at home, in the workplace, at school and when having fun creating beautiful craft projects.

The type of plastic we are interested in is made up of a chemical soup with the main ingredient being Polyvinyl Chloride the same stuff PVC pipes are made of. The finished product is a thin film, soft and pliable and goes by the common name of vinyl.

When working with vinyl you'll see the terms cast and calendered which refers to the way it was made. No need to bore you with the technical details, but there are some important differences. Cast vinyl is more expensive, designed for long term applications and is considered a high-performance vinyl. Whereas calendered vinyl is relatively expensive and is perfect for your Cricut craft projects.

It seems that Oracal has cornered the market when it comes to craft vinyl it's what you usually find in craft stores and comes in sizes to fit most die cutters like the Cricut, Pazzles and Silhouette.

You may be familiar with Cricut vinyl (Oracal 631) which has a matte finish and works well on walls and (Oracal 651) with a glossy finish that holds up well when used outdoors. After reading this book, you'll be introduced to a ton of different styles of vinyl that your Cricut machine will be able to cut.

We've all seen those consumer guides that gather information on products and serves it up to the interested public, after all an informed shopper is a smart shopper, so consider this your consumer guide to vinyl.

When you're searching websites or catalogs looking to buy vinyl you'll come across these common terms; now you'll know what they mean.

Adhesive or craft vinyl. Sometimes referred to as film is available in a wide variety of colors and thicknesses is weather resistant and comes backed with a removable or permanent adhesive.

Application fluid. The solution used in wet applications. Professional sign makers use commercial brands like RapidTac but you can make your own by mixing a couple of drops of liquid dish soap and water in a squirt bottle. The soap breaks the surface tension of the water allowing the vinyl to float on top so you can move it.

Backing paper or release liner. This is the paper the vinyl is stuck too. Don't ever remove this when you put the vinyl on your cutting mat.

Carrier Sheet. It's the backing paper of heat transfer vinyl and uses a pressure sensitive adhesive. It also acts like transfer tape to keep the vinyl in place until you apply it.

Heat transfer, iron on or T-shirt vinyl. This is softer than craft vinyl, so it's comfortable when worn on clothing and comes backed with a heat activated adhesive. Make sure the brand you buy can be applied with a household iron. There are commercial brands that require a heat press machine and your home iron won't do the job, your design will lift or peel especially after it's been washed.

Layering. Is a familiar term to Cricut users and refers to stacking either different kinds or colors of vinyl on top of each other to create your design.

Removable and permanent adhesives. These terms do not apply to the properties of the adhesive but rather to the sticky residue left behind once you remove the vinyl. Removable adhesives like the one used on Oracal 631 leaves little if any residue behind whereas permanent adhesives Oracal 651 can cause damage when removed if left on for a long period of time (more than 3 years) because of the strong bond time creates. So removable does not mean you can peel it off and restick it over and over again nor does permanent mean it will never peel, curl or come off.

Squeegee, scrapper or application tool. Used to apply vinyl and smooth out air bubbles. You can use your Cricut scrapper or any plastic card with a sharp edge to burnish the vinyl to the project surface and make it stick.

Static cling or window film. This type of vinyl does not have an adhesive backing; instead, it relies on static electricity to stick to glass, metal and plastic.

Substrate. Is the project surface the final resting place for your vinyl design, the surface you are applying it to whether it's a wall, glass, wood, metal or plastic.

Transfer or application tape. This is what you use to move your cut out vinyl letters or designs to the application surface. It comes in different styles and sizes and is either clear or opaque.

Weeding. Is what you do after you cut the vinyl to remove all the unwanted, excess vinyl pieces revealing the design.

Weeding tool. You can use a Cricut pick, X-Acto knife, needle nose tweezers, dental picks or a vinyl weeding tool there are a bunch to choose from. Here's a tip save your X-Acto blades when they get dull and won't cut anymore and turn your knife into a weeding tool.

There are a few tools besides your Cricut machine you'll need when working with vinyl. These include:

Some sort of tool to burnish the vinyl to the final surface. This can be an application tool, squeegee, craft stick or just an old gift card. It assures you get all the bubbles and creases out and the vinyl securely attaches to the surface of your project. It's also called a burnishing tool.

A scraper or spatula to help you carefully pull up the vinyl designs without tearing them. Tweezers always come in handy. A pair of sharp scissor with pointed ends. Transfer tape which we'll talk about shortly a weeding tool and a craft knife.

Cricut cartridges, Design Studio, Gypsy or the Cricut Craft room with the designs you want to access.

Because craft vinyl is so versatile enabling you to create endless decorative objects its worth spending a little time discussing its many uses. We'll touch on just a few basic ideas in this chapter to get your creative juices flowing and help you realize the many types of projects that are possible especially if working with vinyl is new to you. In future chapters, we'll discuss specific types of projects in more detail.

For a child's room or nursery, the ideas are endless. You can do animals, toys or even just brightly colored shapes. Put their favorite cartoon characters on their wall or crib.

Teach preschoolers how to count, learn their ABC's or recognize colors with the help of vinyl decorations.

Lettering is another versatile use for craft vinyl. Even teenagers enjoy having their name on their wall, laptop or cell phone case.

You may want to advertise your business on your vehicle. You can create a magnetic sign or apply the lettering using exterior vinyl on the side of your car or truck. Or you can use vinyl on the inside or outside of your vehicle's windows. Exterior vinyl is recommended for outdoor projects since it has a stronger adhesive and is more resistant to UV rays.

Other uses for vinyl include personalizing wine bottles and glasses for anniversaries, parties or special occasions.

Glass kitchenware is another popular project. You can do flowers or decorative symbols or put the name of what the container holds such as Chips, Flour, Coffee, Sugar or Cookies.

You can take ordinary glass candle holders and turn them into unique decorations or personalized gifts.

You can combine vinyl decals with painted stenciled designs surrounded in an etched border for an over the top glass plague showing off the techniques you learned here.

If you have worked with vinyl and are looking for inspiration and new ideas, then chapter twenty four on decorating DIY projects should keep you busy.

How to Apply Vinyl

There are several techniques used to apply vinyl. We'll discuss 3 popular application methods.

The first is the **direct method**. Cut and weed the image then simply remove the backing paper position your design where you want it and stick it down just like you do when working with stickers. This method works best for simple images where you can just eyeball it.

When working with words or more complex applications, you'll need to understand transfer tape and how to use it for your projects. The tape keeps your cut outs in position and lets you transfer or move them safely.

There are different types of transfer tapes; paper and clear. Paper tape is more pliable and less expensive than clear tape and is a better choice if you are going to do a lot of wet applications, but it's harder to see thru. The biggest advantage of clear tape is visibility you can see thru it and know exactly where your image is going.

Unlike vinyl, you can reuse transfer tape a few times which keeps the cost down. Just lightly stick it to the wall or on the back of the door in your craft room.

Though transfer tape designed for this purpose works best; in a pinch you can also try masking tape or clear contact paper. The contact paper is sometimes too sticky and won't release the vinyl, so you'll have to be very careful when removing it from the image. Blue painters tape can also be used.

After the vinyl has gone through your Cricut and the cuts have been made remove it from the mat. If you used a full sheet of vinyl cut around the image with scissors to make it easier to work with. Now you're ready to weed or remove all the negative (not part of the image) bits of vinyl first before you cover it with transfer tape.

This is where your weeding tool comes in handy. Use it to pick out the pieces of vinyl you don't want revealing the image you do want. Now you are ready to cover your image with transfer tape. Depending on the size of your tape you may have to overlap it to cover the entire image. Watch out for wrinkles in the tape they can cause the vinyl to wrinkle. Use the squeegee and go back and forth over the vinyl letters or image making sure you rub the image well so it attaches to the transfer tape.

At this point you have 3 layers the tape, vinyl and backing paper all in 1 easy to work with bundle. Pick it up and move it to the project you're creating and get an idea of where you want it to go making sure it fits.

Now it's time to remove the paper backing. Start in a corner and peel it back over itself at a 45-degree angle if the vinyl won't release you'll need to burnish it again until it's free.

Then pick up the 2 remaining layers and place it carefully on the surface of the project right where you want it. Lay it down carefully because it's hard to reposition once it adheres. Then use a burnishing or application tool rub the image onto the surface. Make sure all air bubbles are out of the vinyl. Pull the tape off, very slowly, at a 45-degree angle. When necessary, stop and rub the vinyl again or push it down with your finger. The secret to this part is PATIENCE.

If you try to remove the tape quickly, you'll probably tear a piece of the vinyl. This is especially true of intricate, delicate designs.

Here's a tip for those pesky designs that just won't stick. Wait a few minutes to let the adhesive really grab hold of the substrate. Then removing the tape should be easier.

Now we will talk about the **hinge method** the preferred way of applying wall quotes or large images. There is the horizontal hinge across the top of the graphic or the vertical hinge down the center of the graphic. Choose the one that will fit your image. You can also use this method for craft projects that require exact placement, but for now I'll explain how to apply letters to walls.

Cut, weed and apply transfer tape to the letters. Now move the three layered bundle to the wall and lightly tack it in place with a couple of pieces of masking tape. Using a level make sure the letters are straight don't measure from the edge of the paper in case it's not straight **measure from the letters themselves**. If you need to make adjustments just loosen the tape. When everything is level put a long piece of tape on the top edge of the paper, this will act as a hinge allowing you to flip flop the vinyl. Flip the vinyl up against the wall and peel off the paper backing at an angle and cutting it with scissors if it's in the way then carefully lower the letters, pressing from top to bottom smoothing them out as you lower them to the wall.

Use your burnishing tool and really rub the vinyl onto the surface smoothing out any air bubbles you see if they persist pop them with a pin and flatten them out.

If your saying has several words and it's too difficult to work with in one piece cut between the words after you have applied the hinge and flip flop each word rather than the whole sentence. The last step is to remove the transfer tape at a 45-degree angle then step back and admire your handy work, well done!

Here's an important tip to remember, try to **weed your vinyl soon after cutting it**. With some brands, if you set it aside and do other things it makes it harder to weed the longer you wait.

For a non-porous surface such as glass, metal or a mirror the **wet method** works well especially if it's a large image. The application fluid lets the image float allowing you to reposition it. With this method you'll need:

A ruler or straight edge

A dry erase marker

Squirt bottle with water and a few drops of dishwashing soap

Scissors

Burnishing tool

Cloth

Masking tape

First, clean your surface and let dry. You can use a glass cleaner, but vinegar mixed with water works best.

You can eyeball the placement or mark off where you want to place the design with dry erase markers.

You can use the direct method or hinge method depending on the size and complexity of the decal or whichever method you prefer.

Cut, weed and apply transfer tape. Wet the surface of your project. If you are working with a large image you may want to mist the adhesive layer of the design after you removed the backing as well. Use your squirt bottle and application fluid to simply mist the surfaces. Don't over wet them.

Then lay the project down on your surface reposition if necessary.

Use your squeegee to push out all the water and air bubbles. Have your cloth on hand to wipe away the water. Make sure you get all the water out. Pull firmly with your burnishing tool but make sure you don't gouge so deeply that you move or harm the vinyl.

Take your time and make sure all the water is out. Then let the project sit for at least an hour; preferably overnight.

Finally, take a corner of the transfer tape and slowly pull it off the project. The longer it's had to dry the better because the water affects the glue and you need to give it time to set up. Take your time and pull the tape off as slowly as necessary to assure the vinyl is left in place.

If you're working with **reflective or metallic vinyl,** do not use the wet method. The special properties of these films require a dry application.

Layering Vinyl

Another unique way of using vinyl is called layering. This means using a slightly larger image of one color vinyl and then placing a small image of a different color on top. This makes a shadow effect.

Other layering uses are adding specific details to projects. In other words, you cut out the basic shape of a house in one color and then use other colors to accent windows, doors, and other details.

When applying vinyl layers just work from the background to the foreground building the image one layer at a time until you get the effect you're looking for.

If you have created greeting cards or scrapbook pages using your Cricut machine you are probably familiar with this technique.

Vinyl can be bought in many colors. You can make your projects in any color that matches your décor. It also comes in different patterns such as flowers, stripes, plaid, wood grain and animal prints.

Sometimes you can't find the perfect vinyl color but using the layering technique gives you additional options.

You can also emboss vinyl for a realy cool effect. Cut it first then run it thru your embossing machine. The backing paper also gets embossed and instead of throwing it away you may like the look and find a crafty use for it.

How to remove vinyl from car windows, car doors and walls

At some point you may get tired of your vinyl projects and want to remove them without damaging the surface they're placed on and without leaving residue behind.

For car windows, long term UV exposure will cause the vinyl to chip off in little pieces making it harder to remove. If you can park the car in the sun and heat up the vinyl you may be able to peel it off with your hands. If you're in an area that is currently cold; use a blow dryer to heat the vinyl because it removes easier when it's warm.

Use a window scraper or razor blade to scrape off harder spots. It will leave a small amount of residue. Simply spray on some Windex let it set a few seconds, and then wipe it off with a lint-free cloth. The more glue left behind, the more applications of Windex you may need to use.

For car doors heat up the vinyl and try to peel it off using a plastic razor blade to protect your paint job.

There are a lot of glue removal products you can use to clean up gummy residue like Goo-Gone and Bug and Tar Remover which won't harm the paint. Just a side note if your decal has been on for a long time and you remove it you may still see a ghost image where the vinyl was.

On a painted wall the method of removal is similar, but you have to be careful to keep from damaging the surface and removing paint. It's best to remove vinyl within the first year or two.

Depending on the length of time your decals have been on the wall will determine how easy or hard they are to remove.

Generally speaking, if it has been less than three years you should have no problem removing them any longer than that may require a little more effort and you may experience some surface damage.

Simply start on a corner or edge of the letter and peel it back at an angle to the wall instead of peeling straight up which could lift the paint. Just use your fingernail or tweezers to get started.

A hair dryer set on low and cool can be used to soften the vinyl do not use a heat gun. Heat the vinyl so it's warm to the touch and it should soften the adhesive enough to let you remove it. The trick is not to heat the vinyl too much as this will cause the adhesive to melt and bond even move to the wall making it harder to remove. Move the dryer back and forth a couple of inches from the wall doing a couple of letters at a time.

Some adhesive residue may be left behind on the wall. If you can't roll it off with your fingers, try using masking tape to dab the wall to remove the glue.

If it still remains household cleaners can be sprayed on the wall. It's very important to test any solution you use first to see how it will affect the paint.

Rubbing alcohol will remove adhesives from wood paneling and vinyl wall coverings BUT it will dull latex paint so test first on a part of the wall that is out of sight like behind the couch.

For vinyl that has been on the walls for many years try ammonia, a little nail polish remover or Methyl Hydrate which is a form of alcohol.

If all else fails you can use turpentine, paint thinner or lightly sand the glue off the walls and repaint.

In the next chapter we'll discuss the different types of vinyl and which are best for specific projects.

Chapter Sixteen - Choosing the Right Type of Vinyl for Your Project

Let's keep things simple. There are basically 3 kinds of vinyl, adhesive backed, static cling and heat transfer vinyl. But within these 3 types are an almost endless variety of decorative styles.

When buying vinyl you have a multitude of choices. The type you choose will depend on the project you're working on.

Here is a list of some of the more popular varieties, some of which you may be familiar with others may surprise you. When I did the research for this book, I was amazed at all the really cool vinyl on the market like...

Chalk Board

Dry Erase White Board

Faux Leather

Flocked

Fluorescent

Frosted

Glitter

Glow In the Dark

Heat Transfer

Inkjet Printable

Magnetic

Metallic

Paintable Magnetic

Pre-printed patterns like wood grain, animal prints, marble and granite just to mention a few.

Reflective

Rhinestone

Stained Glass

Static Cling Film

Textured

Translucent

3-D Holographic

From now on adhesive backed vinyl will be referred to as craft vinyl or Cricut vinyl. When trying to figure out which vinyl is right for your next project keep these tips in mind.

Craft vinyl is often classified as indoor or outdoor. It's taking the guess work out and telling you how to use it to achieve the best results.

Two of the most popular are Oracal 631 and Oracal 651. The 631 is considered an indoor vinyl and the 651 is for outdoor use. However, both the 631 and 651 can be used for inside or outside projects. Sign vinyl is normally used for outside projects such as on a mailbox or the outside of a vehicle. The adhesive is stronger and won't come lose in the elements as quickly.

Oracal 751, 851 and 951 are considered high-performance exterior vinyl and are expected to last up to twelve years their made to resist water and UV rays but are expensive and a bit of an overkill for crafters.

So you're telling me I can't use interior vinyl outside, right? Wrong, you can. The thing to keep in mind is it will not last as long or hold up as well as exterior vinyl. It will crack, fade and peel quicker.

With that said feel free to use your outdoor vinyl to decorate your home decor items like glass, wood or plastic, with one exception. **Do not use it** for wall quotes or sayings as the strong adhesive could literally pull the paint or plaster right off the wall when removed.

Sample packs - This is a good way to buy several types of vinyl at a reasonable price so you can try them out.

Keep in mind that these packs sometimes contain vinyl of different thicknesses. So just when you think you have the settings perfect, you discover the new sheet of vinyl you're working with is slightly thicker or thinner which may require an adjustment in depth.

Saving money on vinyl

Be sure and do a little surfing online for the best vinyl prices. Sometimes Amazon, eBay or other craft sites offer lower prices than the Cricut store. But make sure you're comparing the same types of vinyl.

Here are some other sites that offer craft vinyl at discount prices.

expressionsvinyl.com

craftvinyl.com

myvinyldirect.com

cricutdiecuttingmachine.com

Vinyl comes in sheets or rolls. You can often save money by buying in rolls which are usually 24" wide and need to be cut to fit your machine. Ask the seller if he will cut it for you.

If there is a sign shop close by maybe you can buy your rolls from him since he buys in bulk, he may be willing to give you a good price. Before you purchase an entire roll; try to test the type of vinyl using a single piece. You don't want to be stuck with a large roll that doesn't work well for your projects.

Not every Cricut crafter uses enough vinyl to warrant buying rolls so ask your local sign shops if they are willing to sell you the vinyl scraps they have from large projects.

Chapter Seventeen - Tips for Cutting Vinyl on Your Cricut Machine

This is often the tricky part. When you first start working with vinyl you'll probably ruin a few sheets with cuts that are too deep and cut into the backing or too shallow and won't lift off without tearing.

I'm going to tell you the settings that I use for craft vinyl. However, you may need to adjust if you're working with thicker sheets or different types of vinyl.

The secret to cutting most vinyl projects is to not cut through the backing. This is called a "kiss cut." It barely grazes the top of the vinyl cutting through the film layer but not the paper backing.

This isn't always true, though. If you're cutting a stencil, you may choose to cut all the way through the vinyl and the backing. But we'll talk about that more in a future chapter.

Put you vinyl paper side down on the mat and use these settings.

I set my blade depth on 3

Pressure at 3

And speed at 3

For thicker types of vinyl you may need to adjust the settings slightly. These are just the ones I've found work best for me. Each brand of vinyl is different. Start with the settings I suggested and then make slight changes until you find the perfect cut for your machine.

Cutting vinyl can be tricky for several reasons like the age of the vinyl, is the blade dull or dirty and the condition of the mat. The thickness of the vinyl is also a factor as well as the brand. Use small test cuts so you don't waste a lot of vinyl if you're having problems.

Vinyl scraps from sign companies are sometimes **thicker than craft vinyl** so you'll need to adjust for deeper cuts. If the vinyl refuses to cut well and the backing is coming loose, the vinyl may be old. Return it to the retailer for a refund.

Use the paper saver button to conserve vinyl or move your blade to make your cuts near the edges and sides of the sheets. This will allow you to use the rest of the vinyl sheet on another project.

Try to keep the blade free from debris. Sometimes just cleaning the blades will correct cutting problems especially if you have adhesive buildup on the tip from cutting vinyl. This is also true of the mat. If you have fibers stuck to the mat from another project it will hinder getting accurate cuts on new projects.

If you're still having problems cutting your vinyl it might be time to replace the blade in your Cricut. Try adjusting your pressure and depth first, if that doesn't work try new blades. If the vinyl is moving while being cut use a new mat or restick the old one. There can also be a problem if your mat has deep cut marks in it from previous projects.

Another problem that results in poor cuts is using cheap unknown brands. If you continue to have problems try the Cricut vinyl (Oracal) and see if you get better results.

I always try to store my vinyl in plastic containers unless I'm using it quickly. This protects it from dust or lint settling on the vinyl and interfering with the cutting process.

I also prefer to store vinyl in flat sheets. Some vinyl rolls will lay flat when unrolled and others tend to maintain the rounded form. This makes cutting difficult.

For this reason I wouldn't suggest storing rolls for extended periods of time without use. You can always go ahead and cut mat size squares so they'll be ready for immediate use and you can store them flat. Again, with some rolls this isn't necessary.

I never store vinyl for more than two years after that it can start to lose its flexibility. Also, the adhesive will start to lose strength.

Chapter Eighteen - Wall Art Made Simple

Wall art is an inexpensive way to decorate your home or office and offers a variety of options for any living space limited only by your imagination. It can add a visual impact to any room at a fraction of the cost of framed art.

You can use designs such as flowers, trees, animals, abstract designs and patterns, geometric shapes any image you want from your cartridges.

Or you can use a quote or an inspirational saying that expresses your thoughts. (See Chapter Twenty Seven for over 100 wall quotes you can use for inspiration.)

Kitchen decals are also popular. These include:

Fruit and vegetable shapes

Wine bottles

Tea cups and tea pots

Butterflies

Flowers

Types of food like pies or cookies

There are a multitude of different options for children's rooms which include:

Animals

Cartoon figures

Sports teams

School logos or mascots

Kid's names

Quotes

Murals

Super heroes

Peace signs

Names of popular bands or TV and movie stars

A lot of these designs will also work well for a dorm room when a student doesn't have a big decorating budget. Or if you're an apartment dweller and your landlord won't let you hang pictures on the wall.

Most people use a craft vinyl with a matte finish for wall quotes because it looks like custom hand painted lettering. But if you want more than plain black letters try patterned, metallic, textured or glitter vinyl for your letters and layer them to get that WOW effect.

When working with letters keep this in mind, **the bolder the font the smaller the size you can choose**. The real delicate scripts rip and stretch and are harder to work with. To get the best results keep your letters at least 1/2" and not less than 1/3" when cutting vinyl letters. Did you know that many image cartridges also include fonts so you don't have to buy font cartridges unless you want too?

It is not necessary to weld your letters together unless that is the look you want, like with cursive script cartridges. Using transfer tape will keep your letters straight and in place until you apply them. In case you're not familiar with the term welding is when you connect the letters together so they all cut out in one piece. Some cartridges have words or sayings already welded, but for the most part you have to do it yourself. You can use the Gypsy, Design Studio software or the Cricut Craft room to weld letters together.

Prepping your walls to avoid problem applications

Never apply vinyl to newly painted walls. Wait at least 3-4 weeks to allow the paint to cure and the gasses to escape or your decals will be filled with bubbles. It's not unusual to see bubbles crop up weeks after your installation just smooth them out or pop them with a pin and eventually they will go away.

It's also vital that you clean your wall and remove all dirt, grease or smoke build up. Inspect the wall to see if there are any dents, gouges, peeling or chipped paint as these will cause trouble.

If you have applied the vinyl correctly and no matter what you do it just won't stick to the wall, it may not be your fault. Some premium paints have additives to make them stain resistant which interferes with the glue. Also vinyl will not stick to some types of glazes. Satin finish and flat matte paint may also cause you trouble.

To avoid frustration do not apply vinyl lettering to these surfaces as well which include brick, cinder block, concrete, heavily textured surfaces, leather, oxidized peeling paint, plaster, stucco, wood paneling, raw wood, unpainted metal and wallpaper.

Applying vinyl wall decals is not complicated. Here are the step by step directions to make the process as simple as possible.

Choose the design you want to use on your Cricut. If you're doing a quote you'll probably have to cut the words in several sections rather than one long sentence. Make sure you use the same font and size for each word.

Cut the vinyl using a "kiss cut." You want the vinyl cut but not the backing.

Remove or weed the negative pieces from your cut sheet of vinyl. Apply transfer tape to the lettering. Clean and dry the wall surface.

Make light marks with pencil on the wall so you're sure your design will be placed in exactly the right spot. You want it to be level and centered correctly (remember measure from the letters not the edge of the paper). Some people prefer to use a level rather than eyeballing it to assure the art is level. This is usually more important with lettering than just a single image.

Use the hinge method discussed in the first chapter securing the transfer tape with your letters and backing paper to the wall. Cut between the words making it easier to work with if necessary.

Flip the letters up and remove the backing on an angle. Flop them down and use an application tool to adhere the vinyl to the wall smoothing out all the bubbles.

Remove transfer tape slowly and carefully at a 45-degree angle. If the vinyl letters start to come off, then use the application tool again. Erase any placement marks you made.

Note: If vinyl lettering is removed within the first couple of years it should remove easily. After three years it will often leave a residue on the wall or damage the paint.

When you become an expert at installing vinyl lettering on walls why not offer that service as a gift. Just create the saying or inspirational quote and install it on your friend's wall. Or better yet start your own vinyl lettering business.

I have included short videos with step by step instructions. See the video tutorial chapter for added help.

Chapter Nineteen - Glass Etching Do's and Don'ts

I've enjoyed many of the projects I do with vinyl. One of my favorites is glass etching. With this technique you can make lovely personalized gifts and fabulous home accents.

I recently made a set of wine glasses for my niece and nephew who were getting married. I stenciled each of their names on the glasses using the method I'm about to tell you. They used the glasses at their wedding reception.

In a later chapter we're going to talk about ways you can make money selling your vinyl crafts. Personalized glass etchings are one of the best products to sell.

For glass etching you'll be cutting out a stencil for the design you want.

I like to use the Storybook cartridge for lettering, but you can use any design you choose that fits on the glass container you're etching. Be careful about pulling the stencil around curves or corners. This can sometimes make the stencil bubble or distort the design. We'll talk even more about this later. The point is to use smaller designs when possible.

I use a blade depth of 3

Pressure at 3

And speed at 3

As with all settings; you may need to adjust based on the thickness of vinyl you're using to make a "kiss cut."

Then remove the letters to leave a negative. In other words, if you're printing the name SUSAN you don't want to leave the letters on the stencil. You want the empty space to say Susan.

If you like the look of frosted glass try reversing the method and use a positive image. You would apply the letters SUSAN and cover the entire surface with the etching cream. The only part of the glass that would be clear is the letters.

Make sure to leave enough of a vinyl border when you trim your design. That way you can apply the cream and not go over the edge onto the glass you don't want to be etched.

Clean the surface of the glass with alcohol and dry with a soft cloth. Make sure to wipe off your fingerprints as the oil from your skin can interfere with the etching process.

Remove the backing paper and place the stencil on the glass using the direct method if the design is small or you may want to use the hinge method and transfer tape for larger or complex designs.

Continue to apply pressure until all the air bubbles are out and the vinyl adheres to the glass. This can be trickier on glasses or anything where the design is on a rounded surface. Be patient and apply pressure carefully. You don't want the vinyl to move, but it must be firmly applied. If any edges are not secure the cream will seep onto unwanted surfaces and ruin your design.

The best way to attach a stencil to a rounded surface is to start in the middle and work toward the edges. Cut slits in the vinyl so the stencil has some leeway for the curve of the glass. If the slits in the vinyl pull apart, you should cover them with tape. This will keep the area from getting etched accidentally.

If the vinyl refuses to stick to the rounded edges you may need to use a smaller design or font size. It's usually best to try a flat surface for your first etching project. This can be a baking dish or a squared cubed candle holder or even a mirror.

Once the stencil is applied you'll use etching creams such as Armour Etch or Etchall. Martha Stewart also sells an etching cream. I have used Armour Etch with success but some people have complained it can sometimes be blotchy. So you might want to compare different creams to see which one works best for you. I'll talk about the different creams at the end of the chapter.

Use a soft brush, craft stick or a Q-tip to carefully dab on the etching cream. Be careful that the etching cream doesn't touch any parts of your project that you do not want etched. If it does, remove it with a soft cloth as quickly as possible.

Since these products are a type of acid; it's a good idea to use gloves when working with etching fluid of any kind. Be very careful not to rub your eyes and try to keep the cream off your skin as much as possible. Wash it off quickly when you do get some on your skin. Always work in a well-ventilated area.

Let it set according to the directions of the product you're using some need to set a longer time to etch properly while others will start to eat the stencil if left too long.

Then rinse off with cold water. Or if your product is reusable scrape off the cream and put it back in the bottle and then rinse it off.

Save your sink and the environment

Note: Etching cream can harm sinks and counter tops so be very careful as you rinse it off. Rinse off the etching cream into a plastic bowl or tub and add a heaping handful of baking soda to the water to neutralize the acid before you dump it down the drain.

Removing the stencil from the glass when wet is easier. As the glass dries the image will get darker. Stand back and admire your handy work!

Reusable glass etching stencils

If you have dozens of glasses to monogram you might want to invest in precut reusable stencils. They don't last forever but might be an effective alternative.

I have heard of Cricut crafters reusing their own vinyl stencils by just letting them air dry a day or two before reusing them the next time.

Shelf liner seems to be a reusable stencil material. The adhesive will stick over and over again even after getting wet.

The three most popular etching creams are:

Armour Etch - This has been the standard etching cream I've used for years. The smell is strong so always use in a well-ventilated area. It does sometimes have lumps that cause blotchy results. I usually leave it on for twenty minutes which is longer than the recommended time. (See the video tutorial section for a way to get rid of the blotchy results.)

Etchall - One big advantage this etching cream has is you can return unused portions to the jar to reuse. Which means there is less waste and makes this cream slightly more affordable.

Martha Stewarts Etching Cream - This is more expensive than the other etching creams but tends to be less blotchy. Also, the smell is not as overwhelming. It might be worth paying a little more if your budget allows.

For more of a professional grade etching cream try:

McKay Velvet Etching Cream

Vari-Etch

Matronics Professional 30 Second Formula

Not a big fan of etching cream but like the look of etched glass? Well now you can get that same look in a can of spray paint. It gives glass and mirrors the frosted look of etched glass without using acid creams. Just do a search for frosted or etched glass spray paint to find products by **Krylon, Rust-Oleum and Valspar**.

Here's a **money saving tip** for all of us who recycle and have a supply of glass bottles and jars. If you're new to etching or you want to experiment just use the glass in your recycling bins to practice on.

Once I was confident I headed to the dollar store and checked out garage sales to see what ideas I could come up with for etching projects. I turned cheap, plain glass items into beautiful art glass with intricate patterns and created unique personalized gifts my friends still rave about.

Chapter Twenty - Stenciling Like a Pro

Stenciling is a popular way to add patterns to walls, floors, furniture, clothing, glass, mirrors, fabric, paper, ceilings or almost any other object.

You can use paint, glaze, metallic powder, gold, silver or copper leaf, Gesso, plaster, joint compound or molding paste. By using stencils you can take an everyday piece of furniture or a dull wall and make it a unique decorative item in your home.

You use the stencil like a pattern to help you paint a design in a decorative manner. Much like an artist would freehand it. With stencils, everyone can be an artistic genius even if you can't draw.

Stencils are often made from vinyl which is why I added this chapter to the book.

Another favorite stencil material is Mylar. The big difference between this polyester film and vinyl is that it does not have an adhesive backing. It is reusable, durable and resists tearing. Mylar can also be cut using your Cricut; the settings will vary depending on the thickness of the sheets you buy.

When working with stencils, you have options. You can remove the backing and stick the vinyl on the surface of your project or leave the backing and secure the vinyl with tape or a light spray adhesive. The advantage being your stencil is now reusable when you keep the backing paper intact. It is also easily repositioned.

With other vinyl projects you pull away the negative parts of the vinyl. In other words, if you're using a flower you weed away anything that is not the flower and then apply the flower to your project.

Stencils are, of course, just the opposite. You pull the flower part away and leave the negative space. It's the negative space that is the image of the flower that you'll fill in with paint.

When working with a reusable stencil you'll have to adjust the setting on your Cricut machine to cut all the way through the vinyl AND the backing. For a one time use stencil use the kiss cut and weed your image.

Remove your stencil from the mat. Clean the surface of the area you're going to paint and let it dry.

Apply the stencil using whatever method you choose making sure it's placed where you want it. Tape the reusable stencil securely in place you don't want it to move or if you've removed the backing make sure all the edges of the design adhere firmly or paint will get under the edges.

Pat the paint on as opposed to brushing. If you brush too hard you can get paint under the stencil. You don't want paint anywhere except inside the stencil area. You can also use a foam pouncer or a foam roller. You want to apply the paint evenly but assure that none gets under the stencil. If it bleeds just lift the stencil and wipe it off.

When working with paint don't overload the brush with too much paint. You'll get better results applying two thin coats and waiting between coats for the paint to dry.

Don't think you have to use only one color of paint for each design. You can add strokes of different colors or blend them for a shaded look.

Use touches of white paint along the top of designs to give the appearance of highlighting.

Use a touch of dark paint to achieve a look of depth or a 3D shadow effect.

When making a continuing pattern always use at least three or four of the designs in a row. This way you can overlap the last shape and make sure the pattern is even with the same amount of distance between each shape.

Relief stenciling

Instead of a flat design you can add dimension to simulate carved wood or plaster relief decorations on walls, ceilings or doors using joint compound or a host of other products that are easy to work with and achieve extraordinary results.

Using a mixture of Gesso and glue instead of paint will make a textured stencil that stands out from the surface in relief. You can then sand the image carefully to make them smooth and even.

Paint can be added to the Gesso before it's used or you can paint the designs after it has completely dried.

Apply glue to the finished design and then sprinkle sand on top. This creates a textured design. You can use plain sand or colored sand depending on the look you want to achieve.

Favorite stencil projects include:

Borders on walls, these are usually at the top of the wall or in the middle of the wall acting as a chair rail. If you're stenciling walls around a corner, you may need to cut a notch in the stencil so it will bend around or into the corner.

If you like the look of inlaid wood or parquetry floors but not the hefty price try stenciling a center medallion, geometric patterns or a floral border.

Adding patterns on wooden furniture can make any thrift store find look new and exciting. Chairs, tables, dressers, desks and entertainment centers can be given a whole new look.

Glass jars or decorative dishes can be stenciled. Depending on the type of paint you use they may not be suitable as dinnerware so you can't eat off them. Also, painted dishes usually are not dishwasher safe.

Turn that old glass table top into a family heirloom with reverse painting on glass the centuries-old art form you can recreate with stenciling.

Reproduce the antique look of Verre Eglomise by guiding glass with metal leaf.

Create stained glass windows by stenciling using glass paint it's removable on glass and mirrors so you can change the design often.

You can stencil a "welcome mat" on a wooden porch by simply painting the stenciled design directly on the porch. It will give the impression of a mat or rug.

Stencil a design on a piece of canvas to make your own Persian rug or wall hanging.

Canvas tote bags are another project that adds value to what is originally an inexpensive, non-decorative item.

Hanging ornaments make excellent stenciled crafts. You can buy inexpensive decorations and then personalize them with baby names or the names of a couple celebrating their first anniversary.

Dry or relief embossing stationery or note cards is another use for stencils. You make a cut out of the stencil design on cardboard instead of buying metal stencils. This is a great way to make personalized note cards using your initials or a favorite symbol.

Custom lighting can be expensive, but you can convert bottles or mason jars into instant lamps and either etch or paint designs to produce one of a kind collectibles. There are several bottle or jar lamp kits to choose from.

Create imitation porcelain

Not a big fan of spray paint? Have you seen the metallic paint that looks like shiny chrome, antique gold, hammered copper or oiled bronze?

Try using Rust-Oleum Bright Coat for a polished look and Rust-Oleum Metallic paint for a more classic look.

Here's how to turn any cheap glass items into expensive looking porcelain. Just use Rust-Oleum Painters Touch gloss paint in your favorite colors to create faux Belleek, Celadon or Delft pottery.

You can use a spray painted surface as is or add vinyl decorations for further embellishment.

Remember: When painting on a stencil it's best to dab paint on or brush gently to prevent bleeding. You want your design to have sharp, clean edges. You can always practice on paper until you master the technique. With that said the charm of stenciling is that it's not perfect. It's ok if it looks a little funky.

Chapter Twenty One - Decorating Clothing with Heat Transfer Vinyl

Have you ever wanted a T-shirt with a special decal, sports team or really cute saying and couldn't find what you wanted?

Now you can make your own vinyl decorations for T-shirts, hoodies or any other cloth items.

There are different types of vinyl that can be used for clothing. Some merely use a sticky, adhesive backing that you apply directly onto the cloth. This brand does not always stay in place especially after the clothing is washed.

Iron on or heat transfer vinyl works much better. With this vinyl, you apply the design to the shirt and then use an iron and pressure to activate the adhesive to attach it to the cloth.

Iron on vinyl comes in dozens of basic colors. If you're looking for something special try glow in the dark, fluorescent, flocked, patterned, metallic or glitter heat transfer vinyl. You can layer iron on vinyl to create multi-colored applications.

For custom images, there are printable heat transfer vinyl sheets to use with your printer.

Most iron on film works best on cotton and polyester, but these brands work on nylon and leather Siser EasyWeed Extra and ThermoFlex Xtra. No doubt you will find other brands that work well on specialty fabrics when you do your search.

Cricut.com has its own brand of iron-on and printable iron-on vinyl as well.

If you're in doubt as to which vinyl products to buy; spend some time reading the reviews from users. This can be enlightening as to what products meet the user's needs.

Before applying vinyl wash the item if possible. Do not use any dryer sheets or liquid fabric softener.

NOTE: When you're purchasing heat transfer vinyl make sure it's the kind that can be applied with a home iron. Some vinyl must be applied with professional heat press equipment and will never adhere with just a household iron.

Cutting and applying T-shirt vinyl

First, choose the image you want to use on your Cricut machine. I like to cut the image out on paper first and place it on the item of clothing to see if it's the size I want. That way I don't waste vinyl.

When working with this type of vinyl, you need to flip the design or mirror the image. That way it will look correct when you iron it on. **You'll need to spell words backward and then flip them too.** Write the words on paper so you can see how they are spelled when you enter them on your Cricut.

Place the vinyl shiny side down on your mat. You only want the cut to "kiss" the vinyl it should not cut through the shiny backing. **The carrier sheet will act like transfer tape** since it's clear and easy to see where to position it. Cut and weed your image. So that you know some heat transfer vinyl is harder to weed than regular vinyl.

When cutting iron-on vinyl these settings work well

Speed at 3

Pressure at 3

But blade at 2

Always put a piece of cloth or a Teflon sheet over the design before you iron it on. Do not place the iron directly on the vinyl or it will pucker. Do not use the steam setting on the iron.

You can preheat the garment for a few seconds. Iron on a hard surface such as cutting board so you can apply pressure. Rather than ironing with a back and forth motion which can move the vinyl lift and press the iron straight down lifting the iron across the image. Using firm pressure will help the vinyl to adhere to the cloth.

With some vinyl, you can let cool before you remove the backing while others say to remove it while it's still warm. Follow the directions that come with the product for best results especially if you have a corner that's peeling and not sticking.

When washing clothing that I've applied vinyl too; I prefer to use cold water and delicate settings. This is not entirely necessary; I just find it makes the vinyl look nice for a longer period of time and helps the adhesive last longer.

T-shirts are not the only use for iron on vinyl. Here are a few other ideas:

Jackets

Hoodies

Ball caps

Quilts

Pillows

Tablecloth

Placemats

Table runners

Wall tapestries

Backpacks

Cloth tote bags

Banners

Flags

REMEMBER: You want to create a mirror image so flip your design. When applying lettering words need to be spelled backward and flipped as well.

Chapter Twenty Two - Best Beginner Projects

In this chapter we're going to talk about some of the easier types of projects to start your adventure in vinyl.

Static cling vinyl or window cling film is a perfect beginner project because it has no adhesive backing. It is reusable, repositionable and you don't have to use transfer tape which makes it easier to work with for newbies. It sticks to glass, metal and plastic.

Let me point out that there is a limit to the number of times it can be repositioned. It will eventually stop sticking well. (Read the directions for your particular brand of static cling vinyl to learn how to restick it.) Generally speaking when that happens just rinse it off in water let it dry and it will stick like magic again. Save the backing paper and remount your decal when you store it.

Static cling vinyl is perfect for seasonal projects where you'll only have the vinyl displayed for a few weeks. Your kids can help you apply the designs because it's not imperative that they are placed correctly the first time.

For first projects select larger designs that do not have a lot of intricate details. This makes weeding the project and transferring it to the substrate much easier.

Take your time and weed out the parts of the vinyl that are not part of the design. Some static cling vinyl is thinner than other vinyl films so be careful.

As you progress, you'll be able to work with intricate designs, but they can be frustrating for a beginner.

To sum up: Start with fairly low-cost projects so you won't be as upset if they don't turn out perfect. I also suggest starting with projects with a flat surface. Rounded surfaces increase the chances of wrinkles causing the vinyl to pucker. If that happens just peel it back and smooth it out being careful not to tear it.

Write down the settings you used. If they work perfectly then you don't have to worry about remembering them for next time. If they don't; then you can adjust accordingly and not repeat the same mistakes.

Cheap alternatives

Not sure you're ready to use your expense vinyl yet? Try some projects with contact paper first. It's cheap and works on many surfaces.

Don't want to buy transfer tape? There are cheaper alternatives you can try. Some people use masking tape or blue painters tape.

A friend says she always uses clear contact paper. I have used masking tape in an emergency when I ran out of transfer tape and it did work on small designs.

Because transfer tape was specially designed for its use, I feel it works better than the alternatives.

How to reuse vinyl

One of the biggest complaints crafters have about vinyl is you can't reuse it. Once you pull it off the substrate, it's usually torn or stretched beyond use. Well I'm here to tell you I reuse it all the time and here's how I do it.

I use static cling vinyl as the foundation and simply stick my adhesive vinyl cut designs to it. I can make the design a single layer or build multiple layers of different colors, patterns or textures until I get the look I'm after.

When I want to change the look of things I just remove the layered decal and replace it with a new design storing the old one for future use.

In the next chapter we will talk about another beginner friendly craft vinyl.

Chapter Twenty Three - How to Kiss Your Cricut Cartridges Goodbye

Do you want to have an endless source of images that you can import and turn into vinyl creations without having to buy a Cricut Explore machine? I'm talking any design, image, font, pattern, artwork, logo, photo, kid's drawings any digital picture you can capture is now available to you on printable vinyl.

With printable adhesive vinyl you can reproduce images on vinyl and eliminate machine cutting and weeding. You cut the designs out by hand with scissors or a craft knife.

No need to worry about getting the letters straight when applying the vinyl because you just cut the whole saying as one piece of vinyl like a sticker instead of individual words.

Intricate patterns you could never cut on a Cricut machine are now available to you with this print and hand cut option.

There are several brands of printable vinyl on the market for both inkjet and laser printers. There is also printable cling vinyl as well like Papilio's Static and Ultra Cling vinyl. It comes in clear and white sheets that you just print on using an inkjet printer.

Here are a few things to keep in mind. Inkjet printable vinyl will only work with inkjet printers and not laser printers. Printer settings should be on best print quality to produce clean images.

Wait 10 minutes for the ink to dry before cutting unless your printer dries instantly. It will stick to the same surfaces as regular vinyl.

If the brand of inkjet vinyl you purchased is waterproof, you can use it outdoors, but the image will fade in sunlight. For UV protection you can use a spray laminate. For a fade resistant image the laser printable vinyl lasts longer.

The projects you can create with printable vinyl are only limited by your imagination. I'm sure once you start thinking about them you'll come up with great ideas like these.

For a child's room you can print words like toys, books, shoes or laundry and also a picture of each item for younger children who can't read yet and stick them on bins or baskets.

Within a short time they'll be able to read the words thanks to seeing them connected to the pictures! These baskets can help curb the chaos of a child's room while teaching them to put everything back in it proper place.

Kids are crazy about stickers now you can print photographic quality stickers with a desktop printer. Create your own custom sticker, decals or bumper stickers with a favorite image, sports team or photograph.

A star is born! Copy your favorite movie poster and insert your own portrait images with the help of photo editing software.

One of the coolest things to create with printable vinyl is your miniature family. You've seen the stick figures on car windows well why not print photos of family members on printable vinyl cut them out and mount them on paper doll stands. That way you have lifelike images of your loved ones to keep you company on your desk at work, don't forget to make one of the family pet too.

For all you artists

If you can draw then paintable magnetic vinyl is a way to reproduce your artwork. Use markers or paint right on this white vinyl.

To sum it up you can use any digital image and reproduce it on several types of **printable adhesive, magnetic, static cling or iron on vinyl.**

Chapter Twenty Four - Affordable Decorating Ideas Galore

Home décor made easy

The beauty of being able to decorate practically anything gives you the freedom to experiment and after reading this book the confidence to create unique handmade objects to decorate your home.

You'll no longer have to look for those 20% off home furnishings sales you'll be able to create the look you want and have fun doing it.

For the most part these are inexpensive items that you can embellish with vinyl letters and designs. The ease of which these items can be made lets you change your design scheme at the drop of a hat.

You'll never get tired of looking at the same old decor again. You can tweak these decorating ideas to fit almost any room in your home.

They also make great gift ideas too. Nothing says you care or "I have been thinking of you" like a gift with that special someone's name on it.

Also feel free to use any of these decorating ideas to create craft items for sale. There's a whole chapter on how to sell Cricut crafts whether you just want to make a few bucks to help pay for your craft supplies or you become the next Martha Stewart, that chapter is a good starting point.

So let's get started with these creative ideas that will inspire you to decorate your home for less.

Kitchen

Update kitchen cabinets by turning inexpensive drawer pulls into fancy looking handles. Remove the old knob and apply your vinyl decal where the old handle was then re-attach the handle centering it in the design to create a custom look.

Did you know people create *high-end looking appliances* by adding stainless steel vinyl to plain white refrigerators and dishwashers? I was shocked when I did the research and found there was actually stainless steel vinyl. Make sure you check out the video tutorial section for the how to remodel your kitchen video.

Add new life to any *counter top* with granite or marble vinyl. I didn't know this existed either I thought adhesive vinyl was just for crafting.

Now that you've remodeled your kitchen with the above suggestion don't forget the *switch plates and outlets* even small objects can make a big impact with the right touch.

Spice up your kitchen with vinyl decorations and match the design on *tea towels, pot holders and oven mitts* that hang on the oven or center island.

Now you can create your own *perpetual calendars* with dry erase whiteboard vinyl. Just draw a template and fill in the days and dates of each month.

List all your emergency numbers and contact information for each family member and make your *whiteboard* the first place everybody looks to when something unexpected happens.

Create a *family messaging center* using chalkboard vinyl. Post your schedule for the day that way everyone knows where you are. It also serves as a visual reminder and helps you keep track of appointments.

Need the incentive to get all those daily chores done? Just write your *to-do list for the day* on your chalkboard and erase them once they're accomplished.

A chalkboard is great in the pantry. That way you keep a *running grocery list* as you run out of something just write it down as a reminder.

Do you host themed dinner parties? Decorate *charger plates* and the *center piece* to follow the party theme.

The 99 cents store is filled with ceramic items just waiting to be decorated. The next time you have a dinner party send your guests home with a *commemorative plate* that honors the occasion.

Make going green with *cloth grocery bags* fun. Add whatever you want whether it's a money saving slogan or cute food shaped designs to the outside of the bag. Show the decorated bags to the store owner where you shop; he may hire you to customize the cloth bags he sells.

Translucent vinyl works best when decorating *wine bottle lamps* filled with battery operated LED lights that hang in trees or from you patio roof. (Check out the video tutorial chapter and learn the do's and don'ts of glass bottle cutting and how to make your own cheap glass cutting tool.)

Turn your *kitchen herb garden* and those drab *flower pots* into whimsical wonders with the aid of vinyl and trim your designs with beads, rocks, shells and mosaic tiles.

Have you seen *tole painted metal trays*? They're just gorgeous so why not create your own. You can paint the designs on using stencils or use vinyl cut outs.

Create a kitchen vignette by grouping bottles *of herb-infused oils and flavored vinegars* all of which you made yourself of course in fancy bottles you etched, painted or decorated with vinyl.

Give your glass or *ceramic canister set* that designer look by decorating it with your kitchen theme. Don't forget the cookie jar and any other small kitchen appliances you may store on the counter. Instead of standing out they will blend right into you decorating scheme.

Nobody likes doing laundry so fill your *laundry room walls* with your favorite sayings that touch your heart or a poem that makes your laugh out loud that way doing chores will be less or a chore.

If you have a plain white *washer and dryer* add some color with simple geometric designs. Just cut circles, squares, triangles and hearts and use the direct application method. Just peel and stick the vinyl in place. This is a great beginner project.

Keep yourself safe if you jog at night or take Fido for a walk making it easy for drivers to see you. Decorate your jacket and the back of your running shoes with reflective vinyl and don't forget to put some on your furry friend's collar and leash too!

Living room

Make it easier for emergency services to find your home by displaying *your house number* on a decorative plaque, ceramic tiles or a yard sign. You can make house numbers from reflective vinyl that can be easily seen at night.

Bring a smile to the mailman's face when he delivers your mail by *customizing your mailbox.*

Don't forget your *husband's man cave* it can be decorated with his college sports teams, outdoor activities or his favorite movie.

For all of you animal lovers who want pets but not necessarily all the work that comes with them. Now you can fill your walls with *maintenance free companions.* Create a faux aquarium and fill it with exotic fish and sea creatures.

These make believe cats, kittens, dogs and puppies will always get along on your walls. No need for a cage with these feathery friends and even wild animals can decorate your home safely.

Going for that *rustic cabin look?* Then wooden blocks, plaques, trays or even sliced logs will give you ample surface to decorate.

A set of 4 x 4 ceramic tiles can be monogrammed or decorated and grouped together to make *costar sets.* They make great housewarming gifts too.

Glue several tiles you've embellished to decorative ribbon to create *wall hangings.*

Just visit the home improvement store or tile shop featuring *stone and decorative ceramic tiles* to find gorgeous 12 x 12 tiles to choose from. They can be decorated and framed or displayed on countertop easels. The same goes for 12 x 12 mirror tiles.

You don't have to start from scratch you can *embellish existing items* like wall clocks. Add an inspirational quote to the wall above the clock or surround the clock with seasonal designs.

Combine vinyl lettering with physical objects like pictures or

123

mirrors. Put a border of words around your mirror or top each picture frame with a vinyl design or image.

Call attention to the *fireplace mantel* by adding an inspirational saying above it or surround the fireplace itself with formal or whimsical designs.

Apply vinyl words or designs to *decorative candles, glass holders, votive or candlesticks*. Some battery operated *flameless candles* are just plain white so jazz them up too.

Sliding glass doors pose a hazard sometimes if you forget the door is closed. Use static cling vinyl that you can change often and keep your home safe. Let your children choose the designs you apply to make your home decor lively. Since it's a simple peel and stick application, they can install it too.

Wall art does not have to be famous words or poems you can also decorate with images. If you are *tracing your family history* a tree with leaves representing each member of the family might be interesting.

Update the look of your *staircase* by decorating the stair risers. Either apply your designs directly for a long term application or apply them to a veneer of medium-density fiberboard (MDF), particle board or plywood for easy removal. That way you can change the look often.

If you like the idea of wall quotes but want to change them up from time to time apply lettering to *plaques or cloth banners* instead of the walls and hang them like pictures.

Ceilings were highly decorated in the past with murals, geometric patterns and ceiling medallions. Now you can breathe new life into this forgotten and often neglected surface by adding your own vinyl decoration as a border, in the corners or surrounding the light fixture.

If you have *lighting fixtures* like wall sconces put an attractive decoration around it perhaps with glossy or reflective vinyl and watch the shimmering effect the light has on it.

Make your own million dollar Ming Vase by turning a plain white vase into a priceless antique. Just make your own blue and white porcelain design and apply it. Get in the habit of saving pictures of *decorative art objects* you want to copy. Then look for inexpensive items that you can use to re-create the same expensive look.

Dress up your *front door* with festive door hangers or wreaths for each season of the year. Garden flags and ornamental figurines can be given a new look to brighten up your lawn or patio by adding exterior vinyl decorations.

Wondering what to do with the leftover scraps of marble or granite from your newly remolded kitchen or bath? You guessed it vinylize it. Make an *outdoor sign* saying Home Sweet Home Est. 1999, Please Wipe Your Paws or Attack Cat on Duty - using exterior vinyl and display it by the front door.

What does your door mat say about you? Pineapples have long been a symbol of hospitality; why not add them to your *welcome mat*.

Here is how to *add privacy to any glass door*, French doors or a front door glass surround. We will discuss several options. There is static cling window film that is easy to apply since it has no adhesive backing. It comes in a variety of colors and patterns.

For a more permanent application there is self-adhesive window film. Again the choices are endless you can choose from frosted, etched, stained glass, translucent colors and patterns.

You can apply it directly to the window or to clear Plexiglas inserts that fit your windows and door surrounds for and easy to remove and change option.

Reproducing Tiffany-like stained glass windows is a snap with this type of window film.

One of the biggest complaints people have with self-adhesive window films is they are hard to remove. For a quick solution to the problem check out the video on how to remove frosted vinyl from your windows in the video tutorial section.

Bathroom

Dress up your powder room with *decorative towels*; you know the ones you put out when company is coming. Iron on vinyl appliques work well for this project. To make the design stand out use a flocked vinyl it looks good with the nap of the towel. Bath mats also look extra special with a custom design.

Hand painted porcelain thrones or most commonly known as the toilet make of dramatic statement in any powder room. If you want to add a bit of color to the outside of your commode or completely cover it with multiple motifs, give this decorating tip a try. For a complete matching ensemble don't neglect the pedestal sink, vanity, mirror and trash basket.

Shower curtain liners are less expensive that shower curtains but they are drab and boring. But not anymore once you add your decorative images. (Don't worry your vinyl cut outs are waterproof. See the FAQ section for more on that.)

Like the look of frosted glass then change a plain *shower surround* into a custom privacy enclosure. With the help of frosted or etched glass film, you can do just that.

When guests come to visit you always have to tell them that the bathroom is the first door on the right, but when you *decorate your interior doors* with cute words like "Ladies & Gents" or "Water Closet" that eliminates the guess work.

Like the look of marble in the bathroom but don't want the hefty price tag of a stone slab? Take a garage sale find and turn that cheap *bathroom vanity* into a showpiece by adding marble vinyl to the sink surround and backsplash.

Bedroom

Glass blocks come pre-drilled for LED lights and make great night lights or accent lights for any room. Use glass paints and stencil a design for a translucent glow.

Change the look of existing *wallpaper* by stenciling repetitive shapes in a pattern or randomly. Give inexpensive wall coverings a custom high-end look by adding painted accents.

If you make your own *accent pillows,* you can change them often to fit the occasion. As a vacation reminder, a job promotion, well-earned retirement or make your own joke pillows with a funny pun.

What about *lamp shades*? You can apply any design you want to the outside of the shade to instantly dress it up and change the look but what about the reverse side. In the nineteenth century reverse painted lamps were all the rage.

These antiques are quite costly, but you can create a similar look yourself. Apply you vinyl shapes to the underside of the shade. When the lamp is off you won't see the design but when the lamp is lit the shadow effect will look like a cool silhouette.

Did you grow up with those white roll down *window shades*? They are great for making the room dark but talk about dull and unattractive. You now have a blank canvas to decorate. If you want to try your hand at stenciling with paint, this would be a good project to try since the shades are cheap and easy to come by.

Personalize your guest room with *monogrammed pillow cases*. In fancy hotels, they leave chocolate candies on the pillows, but when your guests retire, they will see their name or initials on the pillow and feel right at home.

If you like the look of a *headboard* and want the versatility of changing the look often use vinyl to create one on the wall above your bed. Geometric shapes are suitable for a modern style. Use asymmetrical designs with c-scrolls and shells for a French look. Go for a stained glass or glazed tile look if you want to reproduce the Mission or Arts and Craft style.

To add bits of romance to the bedroom apply vinyl letters to the wall quoting from your favorite love sonnet or poem.

Do you like the look of gold leaf but not the hefty price tag? Turn any inexpensive *mirror* into an elegant showpiece using metallic vinyl of gold, silver or copper. Their satin finish will reflect the light and add a sophisticated look to your bedroom.

Chapter Twenty Five - Personalized Gifts for Everyone on Your List

Gifts for her

Some of these gift ideas can be decorated with painted stencils, craft vinyl or a little of both.

Create your own *designer shoes* by putting vinyl images on the soles of your high heel shoes. Give Nike a little competition and decorate your tennis shoes as well.

Change the look of *liquid soap or hand lotion dispenser* for each season of the year or to match your bathroom decor. They are inexpensive enough for you to change the look often.

Have you noticed how health-conscious we've become? Everywhere you look people are walking around with *plastic water bottles,* but they don't have to be dull and boring. If you take yours to work, no one will ever mistake it for theirs if it's decorated.

Wondering what to do with all those wedding pictures? Copy them on printable vinyl and turn them into a *wedding puzzle.* Instead of cutting the picture into the typical jigsaw pattern cut it into hearts, circles, squares and triangles.

Need wedding or anniversary gift ideas or just want to make something special for your powder room? Then try making *monogrammed towel sets.*

Look for ceramic, glass or metal *figurines* that are mounted on a base which leaves you room to add inspirational or funny sayings.

Turn your plain *umbrella* into a real head turner it will be easy to identify and you're sure to get a comment or two from anyone who sees it. They might even want you to make one for them.

Do you have a collection of cherished family recipes, if not why not contact your relatives and ask them for their tried and true recipes? Then make copies and send everyone that contributed their own collection of family recipes in a *storage box or binder* that you have beautifully decorated with food motifs.

Are you into scrapbooking? Why not collect photographs and memorabilia from relatives and create a scrapbook for them. You can decorate the album to match the theme of the scrapbook. You can also collect photographs from all your relatives making multiple copies of the photos and create a family archive to be sent to each family as a cherished *memory album*.

Here is an extra tip for all you family historians who save newspaper clippings of family achievements. To preserve the memories make sure you make photocopies of the clippings before they yellow and crumble. The acid in the newsprint will eventually destroy the article.

Daily planners are great for keeping us organized but they're not very stylish. Make sure to jazz up your *planner, diary or journal* and make the outside fun or whimsical while keeping your innermost thoughts safe and organized inside. Decorate them for yourself or customize them for gifts people will actually use and enjoy.

Whenever you give *gifts from your kitchen* make sure you decorate the container. That way your gift will look as good as it tastes.

Gone are the days of elegant twelve-course dinner parties but if you still entertain in a formal way then decorate your *dinner napkins* and *table cloth* to capture a little elegance of those bygone days.

Do you or someone you know have a green thumb? Or if you're like me and have a brown thumb the only thing that adds beautiful color in my garden is the *flags and garden ornaments* that are covered in vinyl flowers and butterflies.

Instead of giving baby clothes as gifts surprise the new mother with an assortment of *baby products* like powder, shampoo, oil, lotion and wipes and of course decorate the containers. The hardest part will be deciding on which cute designs to choose from all the possibilities on the Cricut cartridges.

A *memorial of sympathy gift* is much appreciated during the grieving period. It shows your loving concern. A personalized item might include a framed picture, ceramic plate, figurine or a keychain.

Remember *family pets* with a garden flag where Fido is buried.

Gifts for him

Leather bound books are expensive, but with this idea you get the look of class with a twist. Have you heard of *altered books*? It's where you keep the book intact but hollow out a hidden compartment within the pages to hide something.

Reproduce your husband's favorite novel and decorate it with faux leather vinyl and keep it by his chair. You can store the TV remote in the hollowed out compartment that way everyone will know where to find the universal remote control.

Have you seen the price of those *sports jerseys*? You can save yourself a buck and customize his sweatshirt, hoodie, jacket and even the blanket he takes with him to the games. Just add his favorite team logo or the star players name and number to make any sports fan happy.

Turn your couch potato into a weekend athlete with custom gear. Personalize any *sports equipment* with inspirational cheers like Winners Make It Happen or Don't Sit Get Fit. When you decorate his skis, snowboard, golf bag, tennis racket cover or jogging shoes you're showing your support.

Been to the airport recently and noticed how everybody's luggage looks the same? Make his luggage easy to identify with the design that's near and dear to his heart. If decorating his luggage is a bit over the top then create *luggage tags* that are easy to spot.

If he likes the idea of making his belongings easy to spot then don't forget his *laptop, tablet and phone*.

Instead of a gift basket fill a *coffee mug* with goodies on the inside while making the outside good enough to eat with sweet treats like cookies, cupcakes or pie alamode.

Do you have a gardener, chef, artist or photographer in the family? Just match up his interest with a book on the same subject and make a vinyl *dust jacket and a bookmarker*. You're sure to make him smile when he receives your thoughtful handmade gift.

Children are always looking for handmade gift items for dad. They can embellish existing items like *wallets, mouse pads or neckties*.

Give the man in your life an award. There are dozens of *desktop plaques* that you can add a photo and vinyl lettering to. Let everyone know he's the world's greatest husband.

Home brewing and winemaking have become popular hobbies. Give the brewmaster in your life a personalized *beer mug, stein or a set of wine glasses.*

Honor the master griller in your home and decorate a *chef's apron* and *hat* with barbecue designs.

Using exterior vinyl you can customize *license plate frames* to say just about anything. Do a search for license plate frame sayings if you need ideas.

Dress up inexpensive glass, wood or metal boxes into *dazzling jewelry boxes.* If he's always looking for his keys and wants a place to store loose change then these decorated boxes are made to order.

Is there a card shark on your list? Decorative wall *plaques drink costars* and *gaming chips* can be personalized to say Rick's Casino or Bill's Poker Palace.

If you're lucky enough to have your very own grease monkey or handyman *brighten up the garage or basement* workshop with a sign that says Mechanic On Duty All Night or You Break It I Fix It.

Gifts for kids

Be everyone's favorite mom with this gift idea. If your child is on a team decorate inexpensive *sports bottles* in the team's colors picturing the mascot or team name and personalize them for each member. Don't forget the coach.

Do you coach little league or soccer and haven't found a sponsor to buy those expensive uniforms? *T-shirts and baseball caps* can be decorated with team colors and kids names for a lot less than professional uniforms now that you know how to use iron on vinyl.

For all you homeschoolers now you can create *honor student bumper stickers*. They usually say something like "Proud Parents of an Outstanding Student at Home School USA."

Personalized key chains make cute teacher gifts but don't stop there travel mugs or water bottles would be appreciated too.

Does your *kid's backpack* have a way of disappearing? If so make your child's bag personable so it stands out and no one can mistake it for their own. In fact, you can put your child's name on just about any clothing item shoes too. Depending on the item you can make small labels with adhesive vinyl for the inside of shoes for example and soft iron on vinyl that feels good to wear on clothing.

If you have a hard time getting your youngsters to bed at night, try decorating their *pajamas and nightgowns* with Disney characters, their favorite animal or play time motifs so they want to get ready for bed.

Make bedtime fun and educational by *decorating the ceiling* with glow-in-the-dark vinyl stars, planets and our solar system.

Make mealtime fun for those picky eaters by decorating their *glasses, plates, bowls* and *placemats* with jokes, riddles or funny sayings.

It's never too late to teach your children how to cook. Give them the incentive to learn by putting their name on an *apron, oven mitts and potholders* and encourage them to join you in the kitchen.

Instead of those plain plastic containers help your children clean up their room and let them choose the designs shapes and characters to decorate their *storage bins*. This would be a good beginner project that even children could do. Just make sure your designs are small and simple. Since these are just like decals or stickers all they have to do is peel and stick it to the storage container.

If you're good with tools and have a hand held or table top jigsaw then you can create your own *stenciled wooden puzzles*. There are a bunch of patterns available from baby puzzles with simple cut out images like the alphabet or numbers to 3-D dimensional puzzles of buildings, animals and brain teasers. Remember vinyl doesn't stick well to raw wood.

Don't want to use power tools but like the idea of making puzzles. Try this suggestion. Turn any *photograph, clipart or vector image* into a puzzle. Just use the printable vinyl to copy your image and cut the image into puzzle pieces.

You can also *embellish existing puzzles* like the Rubik's cube. Think of a theme for your puzzle using any Cricut cartridge to cut out the vinyl pieces small enough to fit on the squares of the cube.

If you like to sew personalize stuffed animals and teddy bears with doll clothes. You can even start your own line of *personalized doll clothes*. Your customer would send you a picture of their little girl wearing her favorite outfit and you would recreate it for her doll. That way they can dress the same and be like twins.

Make personalized doll lookalikes with printable vinyl. Just copy the child's photograph and turn them into *paper dolls* for girls and *action figures* for boys.

Kids love bright colors so use fluorescent or glitter vinyl and turn inexpensive boxes into *treasure chests* so they have a secret place to hide their favorite keepsakes.

Create your own *travel games* and keep kids entertained in the car. Save your cookie and popcorn tin's to store the game pieces and use the lid as you're playing surface or you can use a metal tray as the game board. Use magnetic vinyl to cut out the game pieces for tic-tac-toe, checkers, chess and memory games.

If you have the 50 states Cricut cartridge you can use it to cut out the states and help your children *learn geography*. If you don't have that cartridge here's what you can do.

All you need is an inkjet printer, a map of the United States, printable magnetic vinyl and scissors. Just print out the map and cut each state out with scissors.

Chapter Twenty Six - Money Making Ideas

Making money with your crafts is not as hard as you might think. First decide whether you want to start a small business or you just want your hobby to pay for itself.

You can run a craft business from your own home without investing in office or retail space. You choose your own hours and types of projects you want to produce. It's a chance to use your creativity and also make extra money.

Things to consider before starting your craft business

There are always legalities to consider when starting any business. They change from state to state and even from city to city. So you'll need to check online for your local laws. You may need to obtain a local license or file for a fictitious name certificate. This shows you're doing business as (DBA) Sally's Crafts or Alice's Craft Emporium.

In the beginning you can probably work as a sole proprietor and won't need to incorporate. You'll file a Schedule C with your personal tax return.

You'll need to track your income and expenses carefully. You will be responsible for paying taxes on the money you earn. But you only need to pay tax on the profits. You can subtract the money you spend on materials and equipment.

Remember: self-employment tax is higher than the tax rate you pay as an employee. Put money aside so you'll have it when taxes are due. You may need to set up quarterly tax payments to avoid penalties. Talking to an accountant is always a good idea since the tax laws change.

To start with you may want to track your income and expenses on a spreadsheet. But when possible invest in software such as Quicken. This will make your job much easier. Plus you can print out reports to take to your accountant once a year. This will decrease his fees since he'll have less work to do.

Starting a sideline business can be time-consuming. It's best if you can get your family on board from the beginning. Let them know how the extra money will take stress off the family budget or maybe help pay for a special vacation. If your family knows what you're working towards they'll be more excited about helping you. Teenagers may be able to work in the business with you and learn valuable skills.

Establish your brand

One reason why Etsy is so popular is they pride themselves in bringing artists and customers together to develop a relationship. So it's your job to tell people who you are and why they should buy from you.

To build your credibility post videos on YouTube that explain the process you use to create crafts. This helps brand you as an expert. Plus, even though viewers might like to learn to do the projects themselves; they often decide it's not worth the time and effort and will click through to purchase from your website.

Always link back to your main website or craft store from your social media sites. Set up your signature to include your business contact information when posting to online forums and in your email.

Keep your business name in front of your customers and make it easy for them to find you. Include a business card or refrigerator magnet with your company info on it with every new order. Include an extra business card and ask them to hand it to a friend.

The customer is always right

Always offer excellent customer service. If someone emails you with a question get back to them as soon as possible.

Package and ship your products carefully. Make sure you add enough to your shipping costs to allow for postage and packaging. You may want to offer gift wrapping for an extra charge.

Ask for feedback. It's the best way to find out how to improve your service. Make it easy for customers to leave testimonials on your web page. A happy customer goes a long way in building your credibility.

State your return or refund policy clearly on your website so there are no surprises for your customers.

Creating projects with your Circuit can be more than just a fun hobby. If you're willing to put in the effort you can build a sideline or even a full-time business while doing something you love.

How to price your products

When deciding how to price your products consider the following costs:

Price of material

Your time

Business expenses for advertising and website hosting

Time you spend marketing your business

Packing materials

Shipping costs

Many crafters devalue their time. Decide how much you want to make per hour. Then determine how much time each project takes you to complete. Add your time into the equation. Otherwise you'll burn out fast and won't make much of a profit.

While you can start your prices on the low end and then raise them; this can be harder than anticipated. It's better to start your prices at a rate that gives you a decent profit margin. Take the best photos possible of your projects. Write compelling descriptions how the customer will benefit from owning your item. Also give exact dimensions and specific details proving your projects are worth top dollar.

When marketing your crafts; always be aware of upcoming holidays. Mark your calendar so your projects are ready in plenty of time for holiday shoppers.

You may think that after Christmas all online shopping ceases for a while. But January is usually the second busiest month of the year. So take advantage of the shopping mentality and get your items in front of hungry buyers.

Remember to create projects for personal holiday such as:

Anniversaries

Baby births

Graduations

Housewarming

New job

Promotions

Retirement

Weddings

People are always celebrating something. Create projects based on special occasions.

Offering personalization can be a huge marketing advantage and can apply to any item like wine glasses, decorative wall hangings or sports teams. These items are considered of greater value if they've been custom ordered and made specifically for the buyer using their initials or child's name.

Don't make a large quantity of one item until you see if it will sell. This is the beauty of an online business. You can always test new projects on a small basis instead of having boxes of unsold items sitting in your garage.

Use sites like eBay and Etsy to do market research. See what's selling and what not to waste your time on creating. Look for hot items and improve on them by adding your own personal touch.

When you find a popular item that sells well then get busy and make more.

During peak seasons you might want to hire additional help. Your own kids are a good starting place, or maybe your friends. You can probably find a few moms who would like to earn some extra cash while their children are at school.

You can show them step by step how to create the products so you're sure there is no loss of quality.

Or you can have them handle the packing of the items or they can help you keep track of your expenses and income by entering information on your computer. It's easy to get behind on these types of mundane tasks. You can often make more money by producing more crafts to sell and outsourcing the day to day details of your business. They can also help answer emails. This frees your time to do what you do best.

How will you sell your crafts

Before starting your craft business decide if you want to sell offline, online or both. Do you want to specialize or sell a little of everything? Are you a people person and enjoy the interaction with local customers or do you prefer the anonymity the Internet offers? The more you know about your business the easier it will be to reach your goals.

Selling online allows you to broaden your market worldwide or at least country wide. You may or may not want to ship to other countries.

You can set up a website fairly inexpensively yourself and incorporate shopping cart technology or use PayPal buttons.

If you decide to go with one of the online marketplaces they will let you build and host your store for free or my charge a monthly membership. I have listed dozens of craft sites later in this chapter where you can set up shop.

Networking with other people can help you get the word out about your business. LinkedIn and other business networking sites like

Efactor, Ryze and Startupnation are places you can look for like-minded individuals who can help you.

If you find a person who knows about advertising exchange services, he launches your advertising campaign in exchange for personalized gifts for his family.

Don't forget to set up your free page on Facebook that links to your website and interact with other crafters and small business owners. There are apps that will connect your store to your Facebook page so you can post and show off your creativity. Just do a search for them.

Whatever social media sites you frequent remember to mention your business and of course pin photos of your creations on Pinterest.

Where to sell crafts online

Don't forget to do your research and see what's already selling online. Like stick figure families that display on car windows, personalized gift items for every occasion, clothing of all kinds not just T-shirts and hats. There are refrigerator magnets for clubs, organizations, business as well as individuals or go green with grocery tote bags. Really if there is a market for it find a way of cashing in on it by adding your own personal touch.

Before you sign up with any online store visit their forums to learn what buyers and sellers say about the community. Are they happy with the site or is there a need for improvement. Some let you build your store for free but charge a listing fee or a monthly membership. Do your homework and find the best marketplace that suits your needs.

Here is a list of online marketplaces where you can sell your handmade creations.

Aftcra.com only sells Made in America handmade products. There are no listing fees for your items.

ArtFire.com is a marketplace where crafter's and buyers come together from around the world to buy, sell and interact. They have an active support forum.

Azcraze.com has no listing fees or commissions just a small monthly fee to list unlimited items.

Bigcartel.com gives artists a helping hand creating on online store and running a creative business.

Bonanza.com claims sellers prefer their site over eBay and Amazon for its ease of use.

Craftisart.com is an artesian marketplace with no listing fees just a monthly or yearly membership.

Custommade.com lets buyers post a custom order that you are willing to fill.

eBay.com of course needs no introduction.

Esty.com is another well-known market center. Their forums and online guides help you set up shop.

eCater.com offers a free web store builder as well as an online marketplace.

Ezebee.com is a small business network and marketplace where you can even post classified ads.

Festivalnet.com lists art and craft shows, street fairs and music festivals which are all fun places to show off your creations. You can search the site by state or month and find more than 26,000 listings.

FreeCraftFair.com is more of a directory offering low-cost advertising options on their site that gets thousands of unique visitors each month.

Glccraftmall.com has a try before you buy option that lets you open a craft shop and list 12 items free.

Handmadeartists.com helps promote their members with free advertising. There are no fees or dues to be a forum member. To set up a shop they require a membership fee.

Icraftgifts.com specializes in handmade items and allows you to import listings from eBay and Etsy into your easy to set up storefront.

Imadeitmarket.com organizes craft events and is always looking for sellers to exhibit their creations.

Localharvest.org farmers markets often sell booth space to crafters. Search the site to see if there is a market in your area.

Luulla.com is an online marketplace for small businesses. They feature and help promote your creations on Facebook, Twitter and Pinterest.

Makerfaire.com lists family-friendly festivals earth wide where creative people come together to buy and sell homemade items.

Shophandmade.com is now offering a free store for you to sell your craft items.

Silkfair.com offers a simple store option as well as a custom storefront.

Storenvy.com is a fast growing social shopping marketplace that helps you set up shop in minutes.

Spoonflower.com is for all your designers out there. Just upload an image and create fabric, wallpaper or wrapping paper.

Supermarkethq.com connects artists, designers and entrepreneurs with customers.

Thecraftstar.com is a unique boutique of handmade items where you can list for free but pay a membership fee.

Tosouk.com is based in the UK and says it's a free place to list your crafts for sale.

Unisquare.com claim to fame is that it offers auctions without any listing fees. Storefronts are available too.

Zibbet.com offers a free, starter or pro option when using their site.

For those of you who want to see how they sell crafts across the pond check out these other UK based sites.

Ccoriandr.com

Creativestores.co.uk

Folksy.com

Misi.co.uk

I wish I could add Amazon.com to this list but for now they require that items sold on their site have a UPC or bar code. You can buy bar codes but that would cut into your profit margin unless you sell high-end items. Perhaps they will change this requirement at some future date.

Where to sell crafts offline

Get in the habit of carrying business cards and flyers with you wherever you go there is always an opportunity to hand someone a card or post a flyer on a community information board.

With the advent of desktop publishing you can print your own or visit Vistaprint.com and order 500 business cards for 10 bucks.

Your top priority is to get the word out and let people know you are open for business and ready to take orders. One way to enlist the help of family, friends and workmates is to give them one of your products as a free gift. If they love it they can't help but tell other people about your craft items. Don't forget your kid's teachers too.

Offer a referral program either a discount or a free item when someone refers a customer to generate business.

Make sure to advertise your business on your vehicle now that you know how to apply vinyl letters to car windows or create a magnetic sign for the car door.

Visit local stores in your community and ask them if you can display your business cards or flyers.

Often times sign shops are not willing to do small jobs but are happy to refer people to you so leave your contact info with them.

Think of complementary businesses such as photographers, bakeries, caterers, florists, wedding planners, limousine services and bridal shops who deal with customers planning special events like weddings, anniversaries, family reunions or retirement parties. These are the type of customers that would be interested in personalized gift items you create. Leave them your cards and perhaps they'll recommend you to their clients.

You can rent a craft booth at antique malls if there are consignment stores in your area check them out as well.

Once you have an inventory of products you can set up a booth at swap meets, farmers markets, craft shows even art and music festivals. Visit **localharvest.org** to find farmers markets listed in your area or search **festivalnet.com/indexes.html** for craft fairs, music festivals and street fairs.

Make sure you know of any community events scheduled in your area as you may be able to set up a display as well. Put on a decorating workshop at a community center and show people how to use vinyl. These how-to workshops are a fun way to generate business.

Set up a table in front of your local supermarket and take advantage of the foot traffic.

You may even consider doing home parties.

Seek out charitable organizations and fundraising events to set up shop donating part of your proceeds to charity.

Is this all you need to know to start a craft business? Obviously not but it will help you make an educated decision. There are endless online guides, videos and library books to learn how to start a home-based business.

Chapter Twenty Seven - 101 Inspirational Wallies

Now that you know how to apply vinyl letters to walls here are 101 quotes to choose from. Some will inspire you to be the best you can be while others will motivate you to live a happier life and to succeed at work or play. Still others will move you to make the most of your relationships with family and friends.

And some of these wacky words of wisdom are flat out funny bringing a smile to your face whenever you read them on your living room, bedroom, home office or kitchen walls.

1. A dream is not something that you wake up from, but something that wakes you up.
2. A goal is a dream with a deadline.
3. A house without books is like a room without windows.
4. A kind smile and a pure heart will win over others from the start.
5. A man is but the product of his thoughts what he thinks, he becomes.
6. A short hug is sometimes better than a long talk.
7. A successful man is one who makes more money than his wife can spend.
8. A successful marriage requires falling in love many times, always with the same person.
9. Adolescence and snow are problems that disappear when ignored long enough.
10. Adults are just kids grown up.
11. After all... tomorrow is another day.
12. Age is an issue of mind over matter. If you don't mind, it doesn't matter.
13. Animals are my friends...and I don't eat my friends.
14. Any idiot can face a crisis—its day to day living that wears you out.

15. Being away is fine, but being at home is best.
16. Business opportunities are like buses, there's always another one coming.
17. Chains of habit are too light to be felt until they are too heavy to be broken.
18. Depth of friendship does not depend on length of acquaintance.
19. Don't limit your challenges; challenge your limits.
20. Dream and give yourself permission to envision the person you choose to be.
21. Dreams transform into thoughts and thoughts result in action.
22. Drive your business. Let not your business drive you.
23. Every great business is built on friendship.
24. Every time you tell a lie, a bit of truth must die.
25. Everyone thinks of changing the world, but no one thinks of changing himself.
26. Everything has beauty, but not everyone sees it.
27. Everything is funny as long as it is happening to somebody else.
28. Failure is simply an opportunity to begin again, this time more intelligently.
29. Good coffee is a pleasure - good friends are a treasure.
30. Hate the sin and love the sinner.
31. Sometimes we put walls up not to keep people out, but to see who cares enough to break them down.
32. Humor is a rubber sword - it allows you to make a point without drawing blood.
33. I don't mind living in a man's world, as long as I can be a woman in it.
34. I drink to make other people more interesting.
35. I have no country to fight for; my country is the earth; I am a citizen of the world.

36. I like work: it fascinates me. I can sit and look at it for hours.
37. If we couldn't laugh we would all go insane.
38. If you can't believe it, you can't achieve it.
39. If you don't love yourself, how do you expect anybody else to?
40. If you tell the truth, you don't have to remember the lies.
41. If you want breakfast in bed, sleep in the kitchen.
42. If you're gonna be two-faced at least make one of them pretty.
43. Imagination means nothing without doing.
44. In order to succeed, your desire for success should be greater than your fear of failure.
45. Is the glass half full, or half empty? It depends on whether you're pouring, or drinking.
46. It's never too late to become what you might have been.
47. Just remember, when you're over the hill, you pick up speed.
48. Life is really simple, but we insist on making it complicated.
49. Live as if you were to die tomorrow. Learn as if you were to live forever.
50. Love is an irresistible desire to be irresistibly desired.
51. Love, laughter and friendships are always welcome here.
52. May all who enter as guests, leave our home as friends.
53. May you always have love to share, health to spare, and friends that care.
54. Music is the wine that fills the cup of silence.
55. Never invest more than you can walk away from.
56. Never judge a book by its movie.
57. No dreamer is ever too small; no dream is ever too big.
58. Nothing is so necessary for a young man as the company of intelligent women.

59. One good thing about music, when it hits you, you feel no pain.
60. Only the wisest and stupidest of men never change.
61. Our family tree is full of nuts.
62. Pain is temporary quitting lasts forever.
63. Parents are not interested in justice; they're interested in peace and quiet.
64. People become successful the minute they decide to.
65. Pets are not our whole life, but they make our lives whole.
66. Remember that silence is sometimes the best answer.
67. Remember, if you want a different result, do something different.
68. Rule No.1: Never lose hope. Rule No.2: Never forget rule No.1.
69. Strangers are just friends I haven't met yet.
70. The afternoon knows what the morning never suspected.
71. The best sermons are lived, not preached.
72. The best way to find yourself is to lose yourself in the service of others.
73. The dictionary is the only place where success comes before work.
74. The future belongs to those who believe in the beauty of their dreams.
75. The greater the obstacle, the more glory in achieving it.
76. The greatness of a nation can be judged by the way its animals are treated.
77. The less people know, the more stubbornly they know it.
78. The only people to get even with are those who have helped you.
79. The only way to avoid housework is to live outside.
80. The past is a ghost, the future a dream and all we ever have is now.
81. The secret of business is to know something that nobody else knows.

82. The worst-mistake is to be afraid of making one.

83. Think before you speak. Read before you think.

84. This kitchen is closed due to illness; I'm sick of cooking.

85. Those who cannot change their minds cannot change anything.

86. To be a champion, you have to believe in yourself when nobody else will.

87. To get the full value of joy you must have somebody to share it with.

88. True love doesn't have a happy ending, because true love never ends.

89. Wanting to be someone else is a waste of the person you are.

90. We are not promised tomorrow so make the most of today.

91. Whatever you choose to do, choose to do it well.

92. When a man murders a tiger he calls it sport; when a tiger kills him he calls it ferocity.

93. When anger rises, think of the consequences.

94. When searching for direction, the only way to look is up.

95. Worry is like rocking a chair; it gives you something to do, but gets you nowhere.

96. You are never too old to set another goal or to dream a new dream.

97. You cannot open a book without learning something.

98. You cannot run and hide from yourself.

99. You don't stop laughing when you grow old; you grow old when you stop laughing.

100. You will do foolish things, but do them with enthusiasm.

101. Your attitude, not your aptitude, will determine your altitude.

Chapter Twenty Eight - Video Tutorials

YouTube is a great resource for how to videos. I use it all the time when I want to learn something new or fix a problem.

For you visual learners these simple tutorials will show you what you need to know in step by step instructions.

Cutting Vinyl Basics
If you have not cut vinyl before here is a basic run thru demonstrating how to cut it, use transfer tape and apply your design.
https://youtu.be/uLPCNCTXzrg

Wall Art Applications
Here's how to apply wall art. These are short simple videos that show you the different methods of applying vinyl lettering.
https://youtu.be/cEAIJevzz9Q?list=PLF207566E73AB933F

Car Window Installation Tips
This video shows you how to fix problems when applying stickers to car windows.
https://youtu.be/6ZvahnkLJOM

Removing Frosted Vinyl
Avoid the nightmare of removing frosted vinyl from glass by using these tips.
https://youtu.be/vqI2nEj1vo4

Wet Method For Car Windows
Use the wet method when applying vinyl letters to the outside of your car window. Remember if you're applying the words to the inside of your window they have to be spelled backwards and then

flipped. Otherwise your lettering will be backwards and unreadable.
https://youtu.be/PO9iNQV-hYE

Armour Etch Tip
Want better results when using glass etching cream?
https://youtu.be/AO2qNxalupQ

T-shirt Vinyl Help
Working with heat transfer vinyl for cloth applications is easy once you know how.
https://youtu.be/r-o46JcoRgA

Glass Cutting 101
Give plain wine bottles real aesthetic value. Learn how to cut glass the right way for your etching, stenciling or vinyl projects.
https://youtu.be/sFXngPx3w3M

Make Your Own Glass Cutter
You can either buy a glass cutter of build one yourself.
https://youtu.be/6tNgJKQCl7k

Cheap Sand Blasting Kit
Love the look of sand blasted etched glass but don't want to buy expensive equipment?
 https://youtu.be/eVFji6cQO5Q

Chapter Twenty Nine FAQ'S

In this chapter I want to address the questions I most often hear when working with vinyl and glass etching projects.

Vinyl FAQS

1. Where can I buy vinyl? Local craft stores often stock vinyl. I haven't had as much luck with local stores. I don't know if it's just a cheaper type of vinyl they sell or if they keep it in stock too long. You may have a different experience. There are endless online sources available as well or work out a deal with a local sign shop.

2. Is Cricut vinyl my only option? No. There are several manufacturers of craft vinyl on the market. Cricut vinyl is made by Oracal but here are other brand names to check out like Avery, **Arlon,** Creative Film, Endura, FDC, Green Star, GT5, **LVG InterCal,** Mactac, Siser, Transvinyl Flexx, VinylEase, Vector and 3M.

3. What settings should I use for cutting? I find setting the blade at 3, pressure at 3 and speed at 3 works well for me. But you'll need to adjust for different vinyl since it's not all the same thickness. Also, for most projects you'll want a light "kiss cut" that cuts the vinyl and not the backing. But for reusable stencils you need the cut to go all the way through the backing so you'll need a deeper cut.

4. Can I cut vinyl on my Cricut without using a mat? No. Always use a mat just like you do when cutting paper do not remove the backing just place the vinyl on the mat paper side down.

5. Will vinyl stick to any surface? Almost, for best results avoid these surfaces brick, cement, greasy walls, leather, raw wood, stucco, unpainted metal and old peeling paint. If you're working outdoors avoid applying vinyl in hot and cold weather. For successful applications the temperature should be between 60 and 80 degrees Fahrenheit.

6. What type of projects should I start with? If you never worked with vinyl before start with projects with removable static cling vinyl. It is more forgiving when placing it on a surface and can be readjusted easily. Also, use a pattern that doesn't have a lot of intricate details. This lowers the risk of tearing the design when weeding it and attaching it to its final surface. Printable vinyl is also a good starter project.

7. Can vinyl get wet? Yes. It is not going to hurt your vinyl if it gets wet. However, the type of vinyl determines how water resistant it is. Vinyl made for outdoor signs is more water resistant and can also stand up to the sun's UV rays longer without fading, cracking or curling.

8. Are vinyl decals dishwasher safe? Yes. Just use exterior vinyl like Oracal 651 or 751 and adjust the temperature settings avoiding high-temperature wash and rinse cycles. Eventually your decals will curl. Hand washing will extend the life of your vinyl creations.

9. Can vinyl be removed later? Yes. The longer the vinyl has been attached to a surface and the more direct sunlight hits the vinyl; the greater chance of leaving residue. Glass cleaners work well for removing residue from car windows and other glass surfaces without damage. Painted walls can suffer damage when it is removed if it is left in place for a long period of time; usually three years or more.

10. How can I save money when buying vinyl? Talk to local sign shops and see if they'll give you their scraps or sell them to you cheaply. They may also be willing to sell you pieces of vinyl that they buy on large rolls. Otherwise, you'll need to compare prices from vendors and search for the best prices. Buy in small quantities until you're sure the company is selling the type of vinyl you're happy with. Cheap vinyl can pucker or peel off quickly. You don't want to waste your time and effort producing projects that are quickly ruined because of poor quality vinyl.

11. How long can I store vinyl? I prefer to use vinyl within two years. If I'm not going to use it right away I store it in airtight plastic containers so it doesn't get dusty. The tricky thing is; you don't know how old the vinyl is when you buy it. If you store it too long the adhesive can lose its effectiveness. So I suggest not buying in bulk unless you know you're going to be making a lot of vinyl projects.

12. Is it necessary to seal or add a topcoat to vinyl? No. But you may like the look a topcoat or glaze adds to the finished product. When choosing a clear polyurethane avoid solvent and oil-based products. Look for a water-based clear coat that you brush on. Some aerosol products will cause the decal to lift or curl. Mod Podge is also an option.

13. What if my vinyl refuses to cut properly? Adjust your setting slightly up or down depending on whether the cut is too deep or too shallow. Make sure your blades are sharp and clean use a Q-tip and alcohol to remove any sticky residue. Use a new mat when cutting vinyl.

14. When do I use application sprays? If you're working with frosted vinyl, large windows or mirrors due yourself a favor and use an application fluid. Exterior applications in colder weather will perform better when you use the liquid method as well.

15. Will anything get rid of ghosting on chalkboard vinyl? Yes. Regular chalk and Bistro chalk markers will leave a residue behind because of the coarse texture of the vinyl. Try using a Mr. Clean magic eraser for best results.

16. Is there any iron on vinyl for nylon and leather? Yes. Most heat transfer vinyl works well on cotton and polyester fabric but Siser Easyweed Extra and ThermoFlex Xtra can be applied to leather and nylon items.

17. Why won't the backing paper peel off? If you cut the vinyl too deep some of the adhesive can ooze out and stick to the backing making it had to weed and remove. Here are some suggestions. Try heating the decal by setting it in direct sunlight for ten minutes. Iron the backing for ten seconds with an iron set on low or pop it into a microwave oven for three seconds. Heating the glue helps the vinyl to let go of the release liner.

18. If vinyl sticks to itself is the design ruined? No. If you removed the backing paper and the letters stick to themselves squirt them with a little application fluid and gently pull them apart.

Glass Etching FAQS

1. Is glass etching permanent? Yes. Once the glass is etched it can't be removed. So cover all the surfaces of a project carefully so none of the wrong areas are exposed to the etching cream.

2. What kind of glass can be etched? Both clear and colored glass can be etched. You can use etching to make inexpensive glass items look more decorative. Get in the habit of looking at existing glass objects that you can enhance by etching.

3. Is glass the only surface I can etch? No. Ceramic, porcelain, marble, slate and mirrors can be etched.

4. Can Pyrex dishes be etched? Yes and no. Some glass contains lead or plastic which interfere with the etching process. Test a small area to be sure you'll get the result you want. Do not try to etch over a logo or design already in the glass.

5. Is it hard to etch rounded surfaces like wine glasses? It can be. Don't use a large design that goes all the way around the glass. Be patient when applying the stencil. Make small slits in the stencil to assure it wraps around the glass properly. You need to be sure all the edges are secured or etching cream will get under the stencil and ruin your design.

6. Is it safe to eat off dishes that have been etched? Yes. They are dishwasher safe and do not require any type of sealant or topcoat.

7. Can etching cream be reused? Some brands can. You can simply scrape off the cream and put it back in its container. Read the directions carefully to know if the cream you're using can be reused.

8. Is etching cream dangerous? Not if used correctly and the directions are carefully followed. But it is acidic and can be dangerous if not used the right way. Breathing the fumes is not a good idea so always work in a well-ventilated area and wear gloves for added protection. Keep it away from children and pets. Remember the save your sink and the environment tip in Chapter Nineteen.

9. Can I leave etching cream on longer for better results? Yes. Twenty minutes is the longest I've tried. Armour Etch contains sulfuric acid. You run the risk of damaging the stencil and ruining the design if you leave it on much longer. The caustic ingredient in Etchall is ammonium bifluoride and can be left on for an hour if you want.

10. Etching cream sounds too dangerous since I have small children in my home. Is there another way I can create that frosted glass look? You can use a stencil and frosted spray paint. Or you can use frosted vinyl. The design will be placed on top of the glass instead of etched permanently into it.

11. Will food stain etched designs? Yes. So always etch the back of glass plates and dishes unless they are for decorative purposes only.

12. Will etching cream frost large glass areas? Not very well. For solid etching use an etching dip or bath and dunk the glass into the liquid for a frosted effect.

13. Do I have to use a stencil when etching glass? No. You can freehand your design. Just use a paint brush and paint on the etching cream.

14. Is there anything I can do to enhance the image and make it really stand out? Yes. Do a search for metallic wax like Rub n Buff and apply a little white to the design. You can also use glass paints.

Concluding words of encouragement

Craft vinyl adds a whole new array of projects you can create with your Cricut machine. Don't be dismayed with the learning process. Once you've mastered the basic techniques your imagination will go wild with possibilities.

I hope this book will guide you through the basics and eliminate a lot of the problems I encountered along the way.

Whether you're making T-shirts for your son's rock band, animal décor for your granddaughter's crib or personalized engraved wine glasses; vinyl projects are fun, practical and beautiful.

Plus, you may be able to make some extra money by selling your creations.

Don't limit the possibilities. Use your imagination and get started today.

Have you found any of these tips useful? If so please help me get the word out. Mention my books on your blog, tweet about them, pin them on Pinterest or post in your Facebook groups.

Introduction to Cricut Explore

My name is Maryann Gillespie, and I love my Cricut Explore. But it's been a love-hate relationship from the start. The reason I wrote this book was to save you some of the agony I went through.

Several times I threatened to box it up never to return or better yet, sell it and recoup some of my money.

For several months I struggled to try to get Design Space to communicate with my die cutter to complete my projects. I knew the Explore series relied on an Internet connection and the cloud based program known as Design Space to make those fantastic cuts and without it the machine is useless.

The pile of ruined material plus the anger and frustration began to build up. After all, I was a seasoned Cricuter; my Expression machine had served me well for years, so I knew it wasn't entirely my fault.

So I set out to learn even more about Design Space and gathered a ton of tips, tricks and troubleshooting techniques. That changed my experience completely.

What I didn't know was that my Internet Service Provider had been upgrading their equipment which affected my connection.

Now armed with the knowledge I needed plus a reliable Internet connection I can now say I've mastered my Cricut Explore.

This guidebook will provide the confidence and incentive you need to work with Design Space. Sure there's a learning curve, but I'm here to help.

I'm not some techno-whiz, but I am curious and have a desire to learn. So if you too have a passion for creating beautiful artwork, together we can do just that and more.

I want to help others learn to enjoy their Cricuts as much as I do. It was this desire to help others that inspired my books. My hope is to help you kiss the frustration goodbye!

Important advice for new Cricuter's. If you haven't bought a Cricut Explore yet do yourself a big favor and consider this important information.

1. Install the Design Space plug-in and see if it works.

2. Check to see if your computer is Bluetooth enabled.

3. A reliable high-speed Internet connection is required.

My friend Lisa bought her Explore machine and then learned she had to update her computers operating system spending an additional $119 for Windows 10. Had she talked to me first and taken my advice it might have saved her 119 bucks.

First: Realize your computers operating system should be Windows 8 or newer. It's a design space requirement.

I know some users are still using Windows 7 and have no trouble. But with future updates the older version will probably no longer be supported.

Second: If you plan on using Bluetooth technology make sure your computer is Bluetooth enabled. (I show you how to check for that in a later Chapter.) Some PCs, laptops and tablets already come with Bluetooth installed.

If not you'll have to buy additional hardware and install it providing you have an unused USB port as well as pair it to your devise. You do not have to go wireless to use Cricut Explore machines; they work just fine physically connected to your computer or printer using a USB cable.

Third: Download and install the Cricut Design Space browser plug-in. You do not need an Explore machine to check out the application. Create projects, familiarize yourself with the layout, play around and just have fun. You just can't complete the project without the machine. That way you know what to expect before you make your purchase.

Just remember you're dealing with electronic gadgets that have a mind of their own. Plus you're dependent on the Internet to create and cut your designs. Your Internet connection may be working fine one day and completely unreliable the next.

I know that the frustration you and I experience can be discouraging but when the Cricut Explore works it more than makes up for the downtime.

Chapter Thirty – Let's Get Started

So welcome to the world of the Cricut Explore machine. This machine is a crafter's dream.

There's an endless variety of projects you can complete using your Cricut. You can work with hundreds of materials including thicker items such as wood and leather to create beautiful keepsakes.

The options for images are unlimited since you can now use your own images. To top it off, the quality of the cuts are better than ever making it possible to cut even the most intricate designs. We're going to explore all those options and more in this book.

I've written this book for those who have purchased an Explore machine but may be experiencing some problems. You may be unsure of how the machine works and want clearer explanations.

Don't worry. By the time you finish reading this book, you'll understand how to work through the challenges you've encountered with your machine.

Or maybe you're not having any problems, but you feel there is more you could be doing with your machine. We'll discover some new options you may not have considered and accomplish more with your machine than you ever thought possible.

Perhaps you're not a techie. All the talk of using software and downloading images makes your head spin. Linking with Bluetooth? What the heck?

Never fear, it's not as hard as it sounds. No matter what your level of computer knowledge is you can use the Cricut Explore and Design Space software. And feel comfortable working from your PC, laptop, tablet or phone.

This may be your first Cricut machine or you may be updating from an earlier model. Or maybe you're still on the fence about purchasing the Explore model. You have an older Cricut machine and you're wondering if it's worth the cost to upgrade. I'll explain all the pros and cons of the new machines so you can make an informed decision.

No matter where you're at in your Cricut journey this book is for you. I'll walk you through the process of using your machine to its full advantage creating unique custom artwork.

For crafters, these machines are an amazing tool to create a wide variety of projects easily and quickly. The Design Space software walks you through a multitude of ready to make projects for even quicker results.

As I've talked to Cricut users over the years, I hear many of the same problems. I will deal with those in this book.

The Cricut Explore series broke new ground with these craft machines. If you've wondered whether you should stick with your old machine or try something totally different by upgrading, we're going to talk about that first thing in the next chapter.

Chapter Thirty One – The Explore Machine Series

There are four machines in the Explore series. The body style is the same and they come in a variety of colors from the original Cricut green to gold and pastel colors. There is storage space in the lid where you can keep pens, tools and extra cutting blades. All machines come with registration and setup instructions.

Let's start by explaining the differences between them.

Cricut Explore: This was the first machine in the Cricut Explore line. Its big advantage over previous machines is its dual carriage system. You can make a cut and also score or write at the same time.

It is not Bluetooth ready so you'll need to buy an adaptor to connect to your tablet or phone. You can connect to your computer with the USB cable or with the wireless adapter.

Note: This model is no longer available for sale at the Cricut store but is available from retailers as long as supplies last.

Cricut Explore One: The Cricut Explore One comes with only one carriage that allows you to make cuts. If you want to score or write you'll need to buy an adaptor and then switch to the pen or scoring stylus as needed. If you want to use Bluetooth, you'll need to buy an adaptor for that one as well.

Cricut Explore Air: The Cricut Explore Air is the first Cricut machine to come with Bluetooth built into the system. It contains the dual carriages that allow you to cut and write or score at the same time.

Cricut Explore Air 2: The Cricut Explore Air 2 features the dual carriages and built-in Bluetooth.

This machine's big advantage is its Fast Mode capability. With fast mode you can cut card stock and vinyl up to two times faster than the Cricut Explore Air. It is slightly noisier than the Explore Air due to the faster speed.

How does the Explore series differ from the old Cricut machines?

The Cricut Explore offers several advantages over the older Cricut machines. They can cut a larger variety of materials including leather, wood and aluminum and provide precise cutting quality even with intricate designs. Their dual carriage system allows you to cut and draw or score at the same time. (Except with the Explore One.)

The Explore Air and Explore Air 2 can connect to a computer, phone or tablet by using the built in Bluetooth capabilities. Using wireless technology lets you work in other rooms without being glued to the machine.

The Explore series cannot be used as a standalone unit. While older Cricuts had an interface on the machine, the Explore series must be connected to a computer, phone or tablet and operated through the Design Space software.

You can connect to the Internet and then download your projects to an iPhone or iPad. But you will need an Internet connection to get started.

What are the complaints users have about these machines?

The need for an updated operating system for both PC's and Mac's as well as having to be dependent on online software are among the biggest complaints I've heard about the Explore series. The need for Internet access bums some people out. Having to bring a laptop when going to crops or crafts shows doesn't always appeal to everyone.

What do people like about the Explore machines?

The dual cutting capabilities have been very popular. This saves having to run the project through the machine twice or having to switch from a cutting blade to a pen or scoring stylus.

The ease and quality of the cuts are another valued feature. The fact that a wide variety of materials can now be cut expands the never-ending list of projects that may be created.

The Smart Set Dial on the Explore machine allows you to make a simple turn to point to the material you're using card stock, paper, vinyl, or an option for custom material. You don't have to figure out the pressure or blade depth the machine does it for you.

You can now upload your own images thanks to advances in Design Space. The sleek modern design of the machine is popular with users as well.

Is your computer Bluetooth enabled?

Most new computers, laptops and mobile devices come with Bluetooth built it but let's make sure.

From the Windows desktop click Start and type in Device Manager. Clicking on it will bring up a window look for Bluetooth Radios. If you see it then it's equipped with it. If not, you'll need to buy a Bluetooth Dongle that is placed in a USB port to make your computer Bluetooth enabled.

From the Apple menu choose System Preferences. If you see the option to enable Bluetooth, then it's installed.

How to pair your computer for Bluetooth

At some point you may want to go wireless. As long as your computer is Bluetooth enabled it will be able to communicate with the Explore once you pair it. In the User Manual Chapter there is a PDF for pairing PCs, Mac's, iOS and Android devices with screenshots for easy reference.

As mentioned earlier, the Explore Air and Explore Air 2 both come equipped with Bluetooth capabilities. You can connect to your phone, computer or tablet without adding anything else.

If you have a Cricut Explore or Explore One, you'll need to purchase the Bluetooth adaptor and plug it into the USB port.

Make sure your Cricut machine is within 15 feet of your computer and is turned on. Next, go into your Control Panel on your computer. Locate the Hardware and Software Icon. Under that click Add a device and the system will look for available devices.

When it shows the Cricut Explore double click on it. You will then be asked for a passcode which is usually 0000. Click Next as prompted and your Cricut will be successfully added and the drivers will be installed.

The benefits of using Bluetooth are you can connect to multiply devices and move around without the hassle of a cord. With the Explore and Explore One if Bluetooth fails just buy another adapter.

Some people find the Bluetooth connection to work much slower than the USB cord. You'll probably want to try both and see what work best for you.

With the Air models since Bluetooth is built in if it fails the machine would have to be repaired.

Tip: If you upgraded your operating system or had a system update sometimes Bluetooth disappears. If so do an Internet search for, Bluetooth is not available, to fix the problem.

Cricut Basics App in iTunes

The Cricut Basics app in iTunes allows you to get started making easy cuts and projects quickly using iOS devices. It is not as fully functional and does not contain all the features of Design Space but some users like its simplicity for quick projects. You will need Internet access to use the Cricut Basics App.

The following devices will work with Cricut Basics

iPod touch 5th generation or later

iOS 7.1.2 or later

iPad 2 or later

iPad Mini or later

iPhone 4 or later

Cricut Design Space Software

Design Space is the web application you'll be using with your Cricut Explore. It allows you to edit, manipulate and create custom designs easily.

Remember to use a Cricut Explore you'll need to connect to the Internet through a computer, laptop or mobile device. You cannot use these machines without the aid of the DS software. Unfortunately, you can no longer just pop in a cartridge, select an image and push a button.

Design Space is free to use and is also available for mobile devices at the iTunes App Store and on Google Play.

Design Space is accessed on a computer through the browser plug-in. It's installed after creating your account at cricut.com.

Chapter Thirty Two – Featured Make It Now Projects

Since Design Space is such a powerful program some feel it comes with a huge learning curve and want to learn just one thing at a time while others want to jump right in and learn it all.

So I've written this book to satisfy both groups. Chapters 3, 4 and 5 take just one aspect of Design Space and give you a basic overview. Even if you've never seen it before you'll be able to picture it in your mind and start to understand how it works.

Chapter 6 explains the whole program in detail. This is where you actually follow the step-by-step instructions putting what you're learning to good use.

Your Home page

Featured Projects take all the guesswork out of designing. These Make It Now projects have been professionally created by artistic craftsman specializing in greeting cards, fashion, home decor, kid friendly crafts, special events, parties and celebrations to mention just a few. You can create them as is or add your own special touch.

They're easy enough for beginners and great for people who want to start and finish a project in a short period of time.

When you sign into Design Space at https://design.cricut.com it will bring you to the first screen or Home page.

Along the top of the screen you'll see banner ads that tell you about current offers and discounts. It's fun to scroll through when you have time and see what types of deals are currently available. Use the arrows to the right and left to scroll.

Under that you'll see the option to make New Projects or view your own saved projects. You can click on a saved project image to open it and send it to the canvas to work on.

Next is the What's New which will show Make It Now projects that are currently available. You'll also be shown current themes. This is especially timely when it comes to seasonal ideas.

Scroll through them, search by category, keyword or filter the results. Some ready-made projects are free. Others contain images you will need to purchase to complete it. Once you've purchased the image, you can use it as often as you want.

When you find a project you want to try click on it to reveal all the details. Design Space then pulls up the project and shows a preview that includes:

Difficulty level

Time required

Description of the project

Materials needed

Step-by-step instructions on making cuts and drawing

How to assemble the project

Completed photos

Clicking on the Make It button in the pop-up window will send everything to the mat. Just follow the prompts on the screen to complete the project. Clicking on Customize will send it to the DS canvas where you can manipulate it by accessing the individual layers.

Depending on what type of project or how it was created you'll have to detach, unflatten or ungroup to make changes and then redo the needed functions. Remember to save the project to preserve the changes. Hit the Make It button to send it to the mat and follow the on screen prompts.

Design Space will tell you which paper (or other material) to load first. It tells you when to add the pen or scoring stylus by following the instructions on the screen.

Note: When you're placing paper on a new mat don't press too hard. New mats are very sticky and it doesn't take much for them to hold the paper. If you press down hard you'll have trouble removing the paper without it tearing.

Make the cuts and then carefully remove the material from the mat. Assemble the project according to the Design Space instructions. Clicking Save next to the Make It button will bring up a pop-up window where you type in a descriptive name for the project.

The project is safely stored in DS. The check mark next to the word Public indicates this is a shareable file. If you wish to keep it private just uncheck it.

Tip: Any Make It Now projects that you decide to buy gets added to your image library. These images are now available to be used in your other projects.

Once you've saved a project look in the address bar of the browser to locate its web address copy the entire URL. You can share these projects by email or on social media sites such as Facebook or Pinterest. (For the do's and don'ts of file sharing see Chapter Thirty Three.)

To delete or change the name of the project click on it and perform the desired function in the pop-up window and hit Apply.

Tip: I like to experiment but don't want to ruin the original file so I always save my original artwork and create a duplicate to make any changes. To make a duplicate of the saved project in DS, save it again but this time select Save As and name it something like Kitty Cat copy or duplicate.

How to find your projects

Click on My Projects next to the Save button on the DS canvas to view all your saved projects. Unfortunately they are not arranged alphabetically the most recent projects appear first.

Hopefully, the search function will be enabled in a future update but until then search like you do any Web page by scrolling to the bottom of the projects and use the Find function in the browser. Click on Edit and select Find and type in the name. Click the down arrow until you find what you're looking for.

Chapter Thirty Three – Working with Images

Design Space gives you many options for working with images. There are free images in the Cricut library, upload your own, purchase images individually or with an Access subscription.

In this chapter, I'm going to talk about working with those images on your screen. At the end of the chapter I'll tell you how to upload your own images that you find online or create yourself.

Sign into Design Space. From the Home page you can navigate to the design canvas directly by clicking the main menu (The three lines next to the word Home.) and select **Canvas**.

Or click the green **New Project** button at the top left corner of your screen or the **New Project** + icon. This will pull up the canvas. On the left side of the screen you'll see the following options:

New

Templates

Projects

Images

Text

Shapes

Upload

From the canvas when you want to work with a saved project click the **My Projects** button and scroll through until you find the one you want.

If you click **Images** you'll see previews of available images. These are called tiles. The ones with a green A mean they are part of the Access Subscription. You can select from these images as long as your subscription to Access is active.

When you purchase an image it will say Purchased in the bottom left of the tile. You can continue to use that image whether you are subscribed or not; you now own it.

Clicking on the square grids in the upper right corner next to Filter lets you see a few image tiles in larger sizes or to see more, smaller images on your screen all at once.

It's easy to search for specific categories of images in the search box like cats or types of projects such as cards.

When you find the image or images you want to use just click on them. At the bottom right you'll see a green **Insert Images** button. Click on that to pull the images onto the Design Space canvas.

There are many ways to manipulate the image. You'll see options across the top of your screen. You'll not see the options across the top until you've clicked on an image and bring it into the canvas.

These options include:

Select All: Puts a blue box around every image on the canvas.

Edit: This allows you to cut or copy your images.

Align: Rearranges multiple images when they are selected.

Arrange: When one image is selected its layers can be reordered.

Size: You can resize images by clicking and dragging it to make it bigger or smaller. Or you can use the size boxes to type the exact size you want the image to be or use the arrows to adjust the size. There is a box for height and width.

Flip: This allows you to flip your image horizontally or vertically. This is important when you're creating projects that need to be reversed or flipped like some vinyl projects.

Rotate: You can type in a number to rotate your images such as 90 degrees or 45 degrees.

Position: Use the arrows to move the image in small increments or type in where the image should be repositioned.

Layers and Colors

On the right side of the screen you have the **Layers panel** that separates the image into individual layers.

If your image is made up of many layers you can choose to **Ungroup** your image. This gives you the option to work with each layer on its own to change the color or the function. Like changing the layer attribute (Line Type icon) from a cut to a write.

Color Sync: Takes the guess work out of matching the color of one layer to another.

Duplicate: If you want to make an exact copy of your image just click this icon.

At the bottom of the Layers panel there is a **Blank Canvas** square when clicked will change the color of the canvas to whatever color is chosen.

Below that you have the following options:

Slice: Use this to separate two parts of an image.

Weld: This allows you to connect images or letters so they are not cut apart.

Attach: This has two functions. Use it to fasten a score or write line to an image. Attaching items on the canvas maintain their position on the mat.

Flatten: Use this to turn a multi-layered image into one layer for printing.

Contour: With this function you can remove unwanted cut lines.

On the tool bar to the left clicking the **Shape** icon to add a shape to the canvas. This is also where you select a score line to be inserted into an image.

Note: If you're working in Design Space and you accidentally delete something or make any other action and then say, Oh no! I didn't mean to do that. Never fear. Up in the top left corner of your screen is a curly arrow call the **Undo** icon. Click on it and your last action will be undone. Keep clicking and it will keep undoing your last actions. If you go one too far then click the **Redo** icon to go forward.

Uploading Images

You can now upload your own images into Design Space. This is something users have been asking for a long time so it's a big improvement to the software.

These are the types of files that can be uploaded jpg, bmp, png, gif, svg and dxf. Images are either Basic or Vector.

Basic images upload in a single layer. You can edit the image to some extent during the upload process. These images include the following types of files jpg, bmp, png and gif.

Vector images will upload as they were designed and will separate into layers making them easy to manipulate. These include files in the svg and dxf format.

On the left side bar click **Upload** then click Browse. This will open the file for you to select the image you want. There's also the option to drag and drop to import the file. If you're going to use this option, it's a good idea to save the files in a folder on the desktop so they're easy to find.

To upload a **Basic** image select the file and click Open.

Then choose whether the image is **Simple, Moderately complex** or **Complex**. The description on the screen will help you decide which to choose. Click on your choice then hit Continue.

Now you will need to define the cut lines of your image. When working with a JPG you'll want to remove the background so it shows as a checkerboard or transparent background. You can use the **Select and Erase**, **Erase** and **Crop** tools to manipulate the image. The tool that looks like a Magic Wand removes unwanted backgrounds.

Click **Preview** to show the image with your cut lines. If it's not correct or you see a gray box instead of the image click **Hide Preview** and continue to work with the image removing the background until it appears as you want it.

Now name the image and save it. You can save as a **Print and Cut** image which will save the colors and patterns. Or you can save as a **Cut** image which will save only the outline of the cut path. Click Save when you're ready. Remember to use descriptive names when you save images to make them easier to locate later.

When you return to the upload screen the image will now appear in the **Upload Images Library** shown on the bottom of the screen. To place it in your project, select the image by clicking on it. Add it to canvas by clicking Insert Images.

If you've selected a Vector image you'll be taken through a simple process just follow the on screen instructions.

Save the image using tags and a descriptive name.

Return to the Upload screen and your new Vector image will show up in the library. Select the image by clicking on it and then click **Insert Images** it will be added to your design canvas.

One of the most popular things to do is to convert a cut image to a printable image using the Layers Panel on the right to change the scissor icon or Line Type to the print icon.

You can change multiple layers to print together by using the **Flatten** tool.

Note: Some images you upload will not work as well as others. Design Space has to trace the uploaded image to map out or define the outline to be able to print or cut the defined area. To make the process easier look for images with high contrast between dark and light colors. An image with well-defined lines and not a lot of intricate detail will work best.

Best format to save files

When saving their own files to upload into Design Space, the users I've talked to all prefer the SVG format. They find it easier to work with since it's already layered. Print and Cut projects work well with a PNG since it has a transparent background which requires less editing.

You might want to try working with several formats and see which you prefer for specific projects since they can be edited.

Should you save as a Print and Cut or simply a Cut file?

I prefer to save images I upload as a Print and Cut. If I choose later just to cut the file I can change the function to Cut only in Design Space. However, once I save the image as a cut file I can't bring back all the colored detail it's lost for good. So if you're not sure how you'll use the file in the future; always save as a Print and Cut file.

Tagging Your Files

You have an option to tag your files as well as giving them a name when you save them. Use these tags to identify the type of project, the kinds of images in the file, the name of the designer or any other information you might find useful when you search for the file later.

File sharing do's and don'ts

When you save your projects you have the option to share them with the public. This means other Design Space users can see and use the project.

If you want to keep your project private, then make sure the **Public** box is not checked when it's saved.

If the images are no longer available you will not be able to save the project as a public file or if you uploaded your own images to create the design.

Some files will note whether they are allowed for commercial use. This means you may be able to use the file for personal use but you're not allowed to use the image for a project that you want to sell.

Shared files can be altered. Rename it and **Save As** to keep the changes.

How to find free images that came with the Explore

No doubt your Cricut Explore came with free images, patterns and a cartridge or two. Here's how to find them.

From the Design Space canvas click on Images to see what's available. To the right of the screen you'll see an option to Filter the images.

Click **Filter** and from the drop down menu select **Free Images**. When you click on this all the free images will be shown including the ones that came with your machine. Click on **Cartridges** and filter to find the free ones as well.

When you're working with text the free fonts will show up in the drop-down menu showing all available fonts. When working with Print and Cut use the filter to find the free patterns.

In addition there are free weekly images available in the Cricut library under Categories as well as free projects for each Explore machine.

From the Home page you can either click on New Project or if you're already on the canvas hit the Images icon.

Click on Categories to find Free Images this Week. Cricut sends out a newsletter with free images as well.

By clicking on that button you can then scroll through the free images and insert the ones you want. Be sure and revisit every week to see what's new.

Where to find free SVG files

In the resource section at the end of this book I've listed sites that offer images. Some are free others sell images.

Facebook groups are filled with cut files from other members that are free to download. There are even groups dedicated to Explore users and have a ton of JPG and SVG files.

Searching Google for images

I've heard several crafters suggest borrowing images you find online. It may sound tempting but there are things to consider. Not all images online are copyright free or in the Public Domain meaning it's illegal to reuse these images without the owner's consent. No one wants to be sued for creating a T-shirt with a restricted image.

With that said here's how to play it safe. Use royalty-free image sites like Depositphotos, Shutterstock or Fotolia and read the licensing agreements.

Search online for images with a Creative Commons license (CC) that enables copyrighted material to be shared with attribution to the artist.

Or search for Public Domain images since they are free to use and come with no restrictions.

Tip: All U.S. Government photos and images are in the Public Domain.

When searching Google Images click on **Settings** and go to **Advanced search**. Type in your keyword and scroll to the bottom of the page where it says **usage rights** to find images you are free to use. Click the drop-down arrow and select your license type.

Beware of free clip art sites

Not all clip art is free to use either. Some free clip art sites don't have the legal rights to distribute the images. But according to **openclipart.org** their site is safe because artists who upload images, give up their rights and let their artwork be used freely without restrictions.

Sites like **creativecommons.org** let you search multiple websites such as Flickr Creative Commons, Wikimedia Commons and YouTube. That's right when you upload a video to YouTube it's usually uploaded with a Creative Commons license.

I like to look for free vector images where the artist contributes their artwork without restrictions like those found at **freevectors.net** or at **vectorstock.com** which is home to over

100,000 free vectors for personal use or commercial use with a purchased license.

Reverse image search

Have you ever downloaded a perfect image but can't remember where you got it or what keywords you used to search for it? I have and it drove me crazy trying to find it again.

I wasted hours searching to no avail until I stumbled on the technique of searching the Internet by uploading an image. The website does all the work for you and locates the exact image plus other similar photos.

Google has a search by image site. Just do a Google search for the term search by image and it's the first listing.

For a list of other reverse image search engines go to **reverseimagesearch.net** and scroll to the bottom of the page.

Chapter Thirty Four – Fun with Fonts

Working with fonts can present its own challenges. Since there are many new options in Design Space that makes working with text better than before I decided to devote a chapter to them separate from images.

Design Space software already comes with several fonts. The system fonts on your computer will also show up in DS.

If you can't find a font you like you can purchase and download fonts or search for free ones. I listed a site or two in the resource section where you can purchase fonts.

To get started sign-in to your Design Space account and click on New Project to pull up the canvas.

On the left of your screen you'll see several icons. Click on **Text** which inserts a text box into the canvas. When you type the words show up in the box which can be moved anywhere on the canvas.

On the top of your screen you'll see several options that allow you to work with text. It's set up more like a word .doc which most people are familiar with.

On the top of the screen there is an option called **Font**. Clicking on that brings up the available fonts to work with.

Choose from All your fonts, Cricut fonts or System fonts. If you know the name of the font you want to use just type that in the search box and it will pull up that specific font.

On the left will be the name of the font and then to the right of that you'll see a sample of the font with the sentence The quick brown fox jumps over the lazy dog. If you took keyboarding or typing (for those old enough to recall typing class) you'd know that sentence shows you every letter in the alphabet.

Numbers and special characters are also shown. The font preview is a nice way to see what the font looks like, making it easy to find the style for any project.

Under the name of the font you'll also see the style such as **Multi-layer, Writing** or **Single Layer**. This lets you know if that font will work for your current project needs.

Click on the font you want to use and it will now show in the text box. Highlight the text and change it to Bold or Italics by selecting **Style** in the top editing bar.

You can size the text box by pulling on the corners of the box. Or, by clicking an exact number at the top of the screen in the **Size** option. This is good if you know you want your project to be a total of 5 inches or any specific size width or height.

Another option on the top editing bar is **Spacing**. This changes the spacing between the letters making them closer or farther apart.

If you're still not happy with the spacing of the letter you have another option. Highlight the text and select **Advanced** to Ungroup To Letters which moves each of the letters separately. Also working with multiple lines let you ungroup words line-by-line if needed.

When working with a multi-layer font you can ungroup layers too. Click **Group** to be able to move the entire box at one time again after editing.

If you're using a script type font (that looks like handwriting) you can make each of the letters touch.

When you want the Cricut to cut the lettering out as one piece instead of separate letters you'll need to click the **Weld** button. That way it won't make a cut between letters.

Tip: There is no Unweld button it's used to fuse letters and images together not to position things on the mat. That's what the Attach button is for.

If you're working with a multi-layer font you can go to the right side of the screen and work with the layers of the font. For instance, some fonts have a shadow layer. You can Ungroup each layer to make editing changes.

When you choose a **Writing Style**, it won't cut out the words it will write them using the pen you have in your machine. (If you have the Explore One you'll have to change from the blade to the pen and adapter.)

Change the color of the writing on the screen to see what it will look like on the material when the project is complete. Click on the **Write** icon layer to bring up the colors. The Cricut pen colors will show up just choose the color to match your pen. (You must manually add the pen to the Explore. Choosing the color on the screen does not change it in the machine. Design Space will tell you which pen to add at the right time.)

Now that you're familiar with Design Space it's time to get busy crating your own projects with the step-by-step instructions in the next chapter.

Chapter Thirty Five – Understanding Design Space

If you followed my suggestion in the introduction, then you've already created your Cricut.com account and installed the plugin. If not go ahead and create your free account and download and install the Cricut Design Space plug-in. Just follow the on screen prompts and it will walk you through the installation process.

https://design.cricut.com

Recommended browsers include:

Google Chrome

Mozilla Firefox

Microsoft Edge

Apple Safari

Do not use Internet Explorer.

Tip: If you're a seasoned Cricuter and already have a Cricut Craft Room account use the same login information for Design Space. That way all your previously linked cartridges will be available in DS as well.

If you have a mobile device there is a free Design Space App for both iOS and Android phones and tablets available on iTunes or Google Play. Installation, paring, FAQs, instructional techniques and troubleshooting PDFs are available in the User Manual Chapter as well.

The functionality of Design Space basically stays the same throughout each new version. The layout and button position, for example, changed a little from version 2 to 3.

Design Space will continue to update to fix bugs, make improvements and add features based on user feedback. When an update is available, it will automatically install when you sign-in. So just be prepared for changes some you'll like some will take a little getting used to.

Visit the official Cricut YouTube channel for news as well as accessing their how-to videos. YouTube is full of Cricut experts like Melody Lane, Lorrie Nunemaker and AuntieTay who continually produce tutorials that teach both beginners and experts.

Using Design Space to create your own projects

It's time to dive in and get busy using Design Space. For those of you who are visual learners I suggest doing a keyword search on YouTube and find a tutorial with the detailed information you're looking for to reinforce what you've learned here.

When you sign into DS from Cricut.com, your desktop shortcut or the Cricut Bridge, the little Cricut icon in your system tray next to the clock, you'll be taken to your **Home page** where you can start a **New Project**, see all your saved projects or select a **Featured Project**. When you select either new or saved projects you'll be taken to the canvas where all the image manipulation takes place.

We'll talk about the main icons on the right. Templates and projects first then images, shapes and upload last.

A favorite item in DS was called Set Canvas which is now called **Templates**. T-shirt designers find theses pre-made templates invaluable. But clothing is just one of dozens of items featured in this section.

Selecting a template will send it to the canvas where you can add text or images to personalize the item choosing the size and style as well. That way you know if the text is big enough or if the logo will fit the item before you cut it out.

Tip: The templates make designing easier but aren't actually saved in the project. You might want to add info in the tags like Men's T large or include template in the title.

Click on **Projects** to see what's available by category such as Baby, Clothing, Iron-on or Monograms. Use the down arrow to find free projects specifically designed for each machine.

Click on **Images** and select an item from the Cricut library and click on the green **Insert Images** button in the bottom right corner to insert one or more into the canvas. When you click on the image on the canvas you'll see a blue box surrounding it with four corner icons.

The **X** deletes it so does the backspace or delete key on the keyboard. The **Circular Arrow** rotates it and the **Multi Arrows** increase or decrease the size proportionately. If you click on the **Lock** it unlocks the restraints so you can increase the height or width anyway you want.

Top editing bar

To select multiple items just click on the canvas and drag the box over the items you want to be selected or click the **Select All** button on the top menu.

The **Undo** arrow is your best friend. It eliminates mistakes just keep clicking it until you return to the original design or **Redo** if you went too far.

The **Edit** icon lets you cut, copy and paste. **Align** lines up multiple items when they are selected. Click on **Arrange** to rearrange the layers.

Flipping the design horizontally or vertically is done with the **Flip** button. **Size, Rotate** and **Position** lets you perform the function in numerical increments.

Tip: To see the keyboard shortcuts just hit the ? on the keyboard and a pop-up window will appear. Some of the images might be confusing so as an example look at the Save Project As. The symbols are Ctrl or command + Shift + S. There is also a Right Click function to bring up frequently used options.

The **Grid** can be turned on and off or resized by clicking in the far left corner of the grid, by using a keyboard shortcut or through the Settings panel under the main menu (The three lines next to the word Canvas.) To zoom in and out use the plus and minus symbols in the bottom left of the canvas.

Layers panel

Now let's talk about the **Layers panel**. With the image selected you'll see the individual layers show up in the Layers panel. Layers that are being worked will be a darker gray than the others. With little attribute icons that let you **Cut, Write, Score** and **Print**. There is also an eyeball which hides the layer when it's clicked on.

Keep in mind hidden layers will not show up on the mat nor will they perform any function like write, print, cut or score. The little gray bar lets you move or arrange the layers manually. When you click on the image icon or colored circle it will bring up a **Basic colors panel**. Choose from basic colors or create a custom color to add or change the current color of the image.

You can also change the function of each layer or the whole image by switching between the four icons and selecting a different one under the **Layer attributes** on top of the Basic colors panel.

When you click the **Write** icon you can choose the color of the pen you load into the Explore. You'll be prompted to change pens in the Explore when the writing process begins.

To create unique custom images, patterns can be applied to totally change the look of the printable image. Click on the print layer you want to apply the pattern too. It brings up the Basic colors panel select **Patterns**.

Scroll through the patterns or use the **Filters** at the bottom to refine your search. **Collections** display pattern themes, styles and cartridges. Click on the **Edit** button to adjust the pattern size click the X to save the changes.

To insert a score line click on **Shapes** and you'll see the **Score Line** option remember to attach the score line to the layer you want to be scored. The same is true for the Write icon it needs to be attached to the layer so the pen will know which layer to write on.

The **Print** icon tells your printer this is a printable image that needs to be printed first then loaded on a mat to be cut out in the Explore.

Tip: Temporarily hiding layers can make editing easier especially when working with text.

The **Group** button allows you to group everything together in order to move and resize multiple images at the same time. It just makes designing a little easier and only affects images on the canvas not the mat.

Just select the images and hit the **Group** button. When you're done moving the objects you can **Ungroup** them if you need to adjust individual layers.

Color Sync lets you reduce the number of mats you have to load by consolidating the layers by color. Another thing it lets you do is to match the color of an item without having to know the hex color code.

Just click on the item in the Color Sync panel and drag and drop it next to the item you want to match. When you have multiple items on the layer instead of moving them individually you can move the entire layer by clicking the colored bar on the right of the layer and drag it where you want it.

Welding allows you to combine multiple images into one design. If you have a complex image that you want to simplify you can eliminate elements and create a new design by using the **Weld** button.

But it's not just for images. Simple text can be welded together to resemble hand written script. Click on **Text** and type out your words. When it's selected the font editing panel will appear at the top of the canvas.

Clicking on the down arrow under **Letter Space** will bring the letters closer together which may be all you need. If not select the letters and ungroup them so you can move each letter individually.

If you have a steady hand line up the letters one by one. Once they're in the desired position select them and hit the Weld button which will fuse them together.

Tip: Select the item and hold down the shift key to move in a straight line automatically. This is helpful when lining up letters.

If the design contains layers that you do not want to be included in the welding process just hide them and they will not show up in the finished image.

The **Slice** button is used to cut out one shape from another or to cut text out of a shape much like a cookie-cutter. When working with monograms instead of gluing the initial on the shape, why not cut it out instead here's how.

Click on the Shapes and select a heart. Click on Text and type in your initial. Move the initial on top of the heart resizing if necessary. Drag to select or highlight the heart and hit the Slice button. Now click on the initial and move it away from the heart, click on the initial again and you'll see the white background.

The initial has been sliced or cut out of the shape. (See the Video Tutorial Chapter to learn how to use the slice technique to work with oversized objects.)

The slice tool only works with two layers at a time. When working with a multi-layer image the Slice button will be grayed out. To activate the button I hide layers and slice then hide another layer and slice until the project is complete.

Tip: Slice is grayed out if the multi-layered image is attached or grouped. Detach or Ungroup to create single layers to manipulate using the Slice button.

The **Attach** button guarantees the position of the images on the canvas will match the position on the mat. It's your way of controlling the placement.

For example rotated images need to be attached whereas flipped or mirrored images will automatically maintain their place on the mat. Highlight the images and click Attach. Then hit the Make It button and you'll be taken to the mat preview screen to check your design.
Hit Cancel to return to the canvas. The **Detach** button lets you make changes if needed.

Print and Cut

Single layered images will print as is. For the Print and Cut function to work the image has to be flattened into a single layer which signals the printer to print the image. Even multi-layer images can be turned in to a printable image using the Flatten tool.

Highlight the image and click the **Flatten** button and you'll see the little printer icon show up on the layer. To make changes hit the **Unflatten** button.

Some images are good the way they are others need a little customization that's where the **Contour** button comes in. It gets rid of unwanted cut lines in the design. If there are cut lines that can be eliminated the Contour button will be active when you click on that part of the image if not it'll be grayed out.

Multi-layered images need to be ungrouped and detached in order to edit individual layers. Select the image and hit **Ungroup** or **Detach**. Find the image on the canvas you want to work on and select it then hit Contour. It will bring up a pop-up window. Make your choice and click the X to save the changes.

The process can be repeated until all unwanted cut lines have been eliminated. (For a basic overview of Weld, Slice, Attach, Flatten and Contour in action see the Video Tutorial Chapter. Even though the video is for the older DS2 it's still helpful.)

Tip: If a function is grayed out and just clicking the image on the canvas doesn't activate it try highlighting it by dragging across the image. There seems to be a difference in clicking and highlighting for some options.

Once the editing process is finished simply hit the **Make It** button and you'll be transported to the mat preview screen. Each color of the design has a corresponding colored mat.

Check the icons to make sure you've designed your project the way you want. Let's say you're making a greeting card with hand written sentiment but you don't see the Write icon. Click Cancel to return to the canvas and check your design to see what went wrong.

Mat preview

By default DS sends things to the mat in paper saver mode but you can rearrange the items moving them closer together or rotating them to fit even more on the mat. You can even move them from mat to mat.

When you click on the image on the big mat in the center you'll see a little blue circle with three white dots on the corner of the mat. Clicking on it enables you to move to another mat or hide an image on the mat.

If you moved it but can't see it on the mat it's overlapping the existing image in the right-hand corner, just move it to uncover the bottom image.

To make multiple copies just click on **Project copies** and enter the number you want. Hitting Apply will show you how many mats you'll need filled with material to cut.

Tip: When working with multiple copies sometimes the Bluetooth connection times out and an error message will appear or the Explore will pause for long periods of time or stop cutting. Try working in smaller batches or connect using the USB cable.

The drop-down arrow next to **Material Size** will reveal several options like the 12 x 24 mat.

The **Mirror** is for iron-on vinyl. You have to flip or mirror the image when working with Iron-ons.

Now you're ready hit **Continue** and follow the prompts. If you have more than one Explore machine select the one you want from the drop down arrow at the top of the page.

If you're printing hit **Send To Printer**. A pop-up window will let you select your printer in case you have more than one and the number of copies needed. The **Bleed** icon is set by default. It adds a thicker border of ink ensuring the image will be cut without any white borders showing through.

The image will look fuzzy because of the bleed but that's okay it will print clear and sharp when you hit the Print button.

Tip: The **Advanced Options** on the pop-up window let you access the printer preferences. Select best print quality and actual size for printed images.

When cutting **Set materials** by adjusting the dial on your Explore machine to match what you're cutting. When **Custom settings** are selected a pop-up window will show up where you can select the custom material.

The letter C next to the material indicates it's a Cricut product. Make your selection. There is a search option as well as a Category drop-down menu to help locate all the custom material.

Tip: When working with thicker material if the first cut fails to cut clear through you may be able to increase the pressure. Go back to the mat preview and under custom material click on the drop-down arrow that says **Pressure**. Some materials just have the default setting while others let you add more or less pressure.

You'll be prompted to load the tools if you're writing or scoring as well as the mat. Finally Press **Go** and watch the magic happen!

Using text and fonts

Hit the **Text** button and a blue box will show up on the canvas where you can add text. Change the font by clicking on the drop-down arrow next to the name under the word **Font** in the text editing bar.

A pop-up box will appear showing you all the fonts available for you to use in Design Space. The system fonts are the ones installed the on your computer. Some Cricut fonts are free or available through Cricut access.

You can search fonts by name or use the filter to find layered fonts or writing fonts. When searching using filters make sure to clear the filter after each search that way you'll see more results.

Tip: A writing style font looks like a single line that a pen or marker draws. The style can be changed to bold and italic by selecting it from the Style drop-down menu. If you use a system font and convert it into a writing font by changing the icon to Write it will only outline the letters as if you traced them. The letters won't be filled in with color.

One of the cool features I like to use when working in Photoshop is adding a drop shadow to text. I fully expected that feature to be available in DS but could not find it in the font editing bar. So I started to experiment to see if I could create the effect. Slicing kind of works but I wanted something easier.

That's when I figured out Cricut offers some multi-layered fonts with a hidden shadow layer. To enable the effect I just clicked on the eyeball to unhide the layer.

To edit the existing text just double-click it. Additional editing features include changing the size, spacing and alignment. Under the **Advanced** option you can ungroup the letters and when working with multiple lines ungroup by line.

Now it makes it much easier to increase or decrease the space in between each letter like I previously mentioned when welding letters. When the editing is complete select **Attach** so that the edited text stays in place and looks the same on the mat.

Don't forget to attach the writing to the material as well by selecting them both and hitting Attach. That way the writing shows up on top of the specific material you intended.

An inspirational quote or a favorite saying created in Microsoft Word can be copied and pasted into a text box in DS.

Tip: To avoid scrolling through line after line of text you typed into the text box, click on the little dots in the lower right corner and drag it to enlarge the text box for easy viewing.

To add different fonts to the design you have to create separate text boxes. Each text box will only contain one font style.

Inserting free and paid images

Clicking **Images** will take you to the Cricut library where more than 60,000 images are available for your designing pleasure. Some are free others can be purchased individually or as a digital cartridge or with a membership in Cricut Access.

Even paid images can also be inserted into the canvas and manipulated. When you're ready to cut the image at that point you'll be prompted to pay for it.

Search through images, cartridges, uploaded images and purchased items using keyword searches.

Tip: The search engine is keyword specific so try using both the singular and plural form of the word to bring up the most results example dog versus dogs.

Make it easier to find the exact image you want by filtering your searches and narrowing the options by clicking on **Filter**. Clear the filters after each search for best results. To return to the main page after multiple searches just click the word Images in the upper left-hand corner.

To learn more information about the image click on the little letter *i* in the lower right corner. You'll see the name and number of that particular image as well as the name of the cartridge it's located in.

Clicking the name of the cartridge will bring up all images on that cartridge. That's a great way of seeing what's on the cartridge to help you decide if you want to buy it or not.

You can select multiple images by clicking on them. To see all the images that have been selected look for their small icons at the bottom of the image window. They can be deleted from your selection by clicking their icon.

Click **Insert Images** and they will all show up on the canvas.

Searching by **Category** brings up the free images for the week as well as favorite and newly added items. Plus a whole list of popular categories. Clicking on the category you want to search then type in your keyword to find relevant images.

This is where you'll also find brand names like Sesame Street, Disney or Anna Griffin.

Uploading images

One of the most exciting features in Design Space is working with your own uploaded images. In a previous chapter we talked about the types of images to upload. Clicking on **Upload** will bring up the upload screen where you choose the type of file you're uploading. Choose either **Image** or **Pattern** and you'll be able to either drag-and-drop or browse for the file.

When working with single layered images like JPEG's or PNG's you'll need to select the type of image whether it's simple or complex. SVG files upload as is.

If the wrong file was uploaded click **Replace Image** under the picture and return to the previous screen.

When the image uploads you'll be able to edit it. Use the magnifying glass with the **plus** or **minus** to zoom in or out in the upper right. The two arrows are **undo** and **redo**.

The three editing tools in the upper left are what I call the **Magic Wand** which removes backgrounds. Printers will not print white ink so remove the white backgrounds from the images. The **Eraser** which is resizable and gets rid of any unwanted parts of the image and the **Crop** tool that cuts out the selected area eliminating the rest.

Using the **Preview** button helps you avoid mistakes and see areas in the image you missed so use it often. Click Continue after editing to save the file. Name the image and add specific tags to make the image easier to find when searching for it.

Click on the image to save the file as a Print and Cut and retain all the colored details, saving it as a Cut file will turn any image into a silhouette. Click Save and the file will be stored in DS not on your computer.

Recently uploaded images will appear at the bottom of the upload window. To insert it into the canvas click on it and hit the green **Insert Images** button. To delete it click the *i* and the trash can icon will appear.

Print and Cut details

Here's how to turn a cut image found in the Cricut library into a Print and Cut. Multi-layered cuttable images can be flattened which converts them into printable images. Insert the cut file into the canvas and hit the **Flatten** button. If the Flatten button is unavailable or grayed out check the layers panel for a score line or Write icon and hide them. To keep the same design drag across the image to highlight it and click Flatten.

To edit the design drag to highlight the image and click **Ungroup** to work on the individual layers. Change the color; add patterns, text, whatever customization you want to personalize the image needs to be done before you flatten it.

When the image is ready to be printed and has been flattened hit the **Make It** button.

The same is true in reverse. Printable files can be converted to cut only files. Simple, single layered images can be converted by clicking the print icon on the image layer and changing it to the scissor or Cut icon.

Printable images with more than one layer need to be unflattened first. Highlight the image and click **Unflatten**. Click the printer icon which brings up the color panel. Across the top you'll see the other icons click the scissors. When you hit the Make It button you'll see the different cuts laid out on the mats indicating it is now a cut file.

Problems with Design Space

If you gave up using Design Space in the past because of all the Adobe Flash and Shockwave errors it's time to return. Flash has been replaced by a newer, faster more responsive program.

In the past the most often heard complaint was the software was buggy and slow to respond. The updated version seems to be much quicker.

Happily many of the problems that users had with Design Space seem to have been resolved, or at least improved. Provo Craft strives to provide its users with a satisfying experience and listens to our feedback. Design Space will continue to improve with each new update.

Chapter Thirty Six – Cartridges or a Subscription

If you've previously linked cartridges to the Cricut Craft Room they're saved in your account. If they're linked to the Gypsy just sync you're Gypsy to the Craft Room and all those images will be available in Design Space as well.

You can also buy a group of images as a digital cartridge. You'll be able to preview all the images on the cartridge before buying by clicking on the name. They will usually contain over a hundred images and can be purchased for around $30. This is much cheaper than buying the images at .99 each if you think you'll have use for them. Cheaper cartridges with fewer images are also available.

Tip: When you buy a Digital cartridge it automatically links to your Cricut account and becomes available in Design Space.

When you sign into Design Space all of your previously linked cartridges (from past machines) will be available providing you used the same Cricut account user info i.e. username and password.

On occasion customer service might tell you to set up a new account if you're experiencing problems. If you've linked cartridges to the old account, ask them if they'll combine accounts or make the cartridges available to you on the new account as well.

If you have new physical cartridges put them into the slot on the left side of the Explore machine and link them to your account making them available in Design Space.

Tip: To save money on eBay search for cricut cartridges bundle or cricut cartridge lot. Ask if they are new and have not been registered or linked to a previous account.

Cartridges can no longer be used in the Explore like older machines. They have to be linked first and don't forget to register them as well.

How to link cartridges in Design Space

Sign-in to your Design Space account on a computer not on a tablet or phone.

Make sure the Explore is turned on. Since you want the data to transfer smoothly connect using the USB cable to assure a strong connection.

Click on the main menu in the top left corner and select **Link Cartridges** from the drop-down menu.

From the new screen you'll see Select Cricut Device at the top choose the USB version not the Bluetooth one. You'll be given directions to insert the cartridge.

To the left on your Explore machine you'll find a slot above the Open button. Place your cartridge firmly into that slot with a label facing out. You'll feel it lock in place.

Your computer will search for a connection to the Explore machine. Once it's located click the green **Link Cartridge** button and the software will do the work. Remember once a cartridge is linked it can't be unlinked.

If you encounter problems or you have linked your cartridges to a Gypsy, additional troubleshooting help is available in the User Manual Chapter.

Where to find a list of your linked cartridges in Design Space

From the canvas click on Images to see the options at the top of the screen that says Categories, Cartridges click on **Cartridges.**

Use the Filter icon and select **My Cartridges**. Design Space will then show only the cartridges that you already own.

In the search box you can then type a word such as horse or flower and it will search your cartridges and find the images that match your criteria.

You can also search by the name of the cartridge. It will show all images on that cartridge. But you can then search for all birds on that cartridge and it will show only the images that you've asked for from that particular cartridge.

Used cartridge warning

If you're willing to take a chance, buy from a reputable seller and make sure he guarantees the cartridge has never been linked. If the cartridges have previously been linked to an account they cannot be added to your account and can't be used in the Explore.

If you have older Cricut machines my Cricut Tips book has a chapter on buying used Cricut products.

Should you purchase the subscription?

Another option is buying a subscription to Cricut Access. This allows you to use all the images and fonts that come with that subscription. (To see a list of all the cartridges included in the Access subscription look for the link in the User Manual Chapter.) You can pay the fee monthly or save a little money by purchasing an annual subscription.

This subscription does not allow you to use all the images in Design Space. Some brand name images like Sesame Street or Disney have to be purchased separately due to licensing agreements.

Tip: The Explore machines come with a free trial to Cricut Access. It will automatically expire if you don't want to renew it when prompted.

How to determine if the subscription is right for you

If the shared cut files, online SVG's, your own cartridges and free images in the Cricut library don't provide you with enough design opportunities then you may consider buying an Access subscription.

Or if you're looking for discounts on digital content as well as items you buy from Cricut.com ranging from 10% to 50% off.

I suggest keeping track of how many images you buy in a month. You'll quickly see if the cost will be cheaper with the subscription.

Also, consider that many people use their machine constantly the first month or two then get busy with other things. If you think this will happen, you might want to pay by the month instead of paying for the year.

There are three subscription plans to choose from. The Font plan is the cheapest and the Premium is the most expensive. The standard plan includes 30,000 images, 1,000 projects, and 350 fonts for less than $100 per year. This is why many users find it the best plan for the money.

Tip: For additional savings search online for Cricut access promo code or Cricut coupons.

When you are scrolling through images and fonts besides the green A in the left-hand corner denoting it's an Access item the purchase price is shown in the bottom left-hand corner.

Cartridges can be viewed alphabetically in Design Space. If you want the digital handbook and the list of all Cricut cartridges, even those not available in the Access subscription use the link in the User Manual Chapter.

Chapter Thirty Seven – Useful Tools-n-Stuff

When you purchase your machine except the Explore One it will come with:

12 x 12 cutting mat

German carbide cutting blade and housing

USB cord

Power cord

Silver pen

Handy storage tote

Getting started guide

Sample materials for the first project

After you've worked with your Cricut for a while you might want to add some of the following accessories. You can purchase them at Cricut.com, Amazon, eBay, HSN or at local craft stores.

Mats

12 x 24 mat – this is used for cutting larger projects. Mats come in a variety of stickiness.

Green – standard mat used for most materials

Blue – light grip mat used for materials such as thin paper that tare easily.

Purple – Strong grip mat for thick materials such as wood, leather or heavy card stock.

FabricGrip Mat – It's specially designed to hold fabrics firmly.

As you use your mats they will naturally become less sticky. So if you prefer not to purchase different kinds of mats just use older mats for projects that require less stickiness. Tape can also be used on the side to secure material in place.

Blades

Your machine comes with one German carbide blade. This is a new type of blade and works better and lasts longer than the previous Cricut blades. In my Cricut Tips book I recommend these blades years ago and suggested alternate brands for additional savings.

Some crafters prefer to switch blades for use with different materials. These are the same type blades; they just reserve them for specific materials, one for vinyl, one for paper, one for fabric. This is purely a personal preference but some say it improves the quality of their cuts over time and extends the life of the blades.

You'll definitely want to have at least one spare blade ready in advance. You don't want to be working on a major project and then find your blade is too dull to make precise cuts.

You can use the regular Cricut replacement blade instead of the German carbide blade. However, it was not designed for the Explore machines and will not produce optimal results. The slant of the blade is slightly different and the cutting edge is not as good. It will not maintain its sharp edge as long as the German carbide brand.

Another blade option is the Deep Cut blade. This is used for thicker material. You'll need to buy not only the blade but the housing, as well.

Pens

Since the Explore One only has one accessory carriage, you have to switch out the blade housing and insert the pen and adapter. This accessory adapter is different from the one for the Explore Air machines. When buying supplies be specific in your searches and get the right products designed for your specific Explore machine.

You may want to have a selection of pens in a variety of colors for writing on your projects. Along with the pens purchased from Cricut, the following work well and are usually much cheaper.

Pilot Precise V5 Pens

American Crafts Precision Pens, Glitter Markers, Galaxy Markers, and Slick Writers

Recollections Markers

Crayola Thin Tips

Believe it or not, even a Bic ballpoint pen will write in Explore machines with the help of a homemade multi pen adapter. Some do-it-yourselfer came up with what looks like a piece of PVC with a set screw and sells them on eBay and Amazon. It makes any pen or marker fit the Explore.

The adapter works with all the Explore machines except the Explore One. Just do a search for Cricut Explore multi pen adapter or make your own.

Scrapers

This tool is used to gently scrape left over material from the cutting mat. This should be done after every use to keep the mat clean.

Spatulas

Are used to help remove projects from the mat to prevent tearing. The spatula is carefully slid under the material that has been cut to help lift it off the mat.

There are different ones available. The users I've talked to prefer the thinner spatulas when working with delicate materials.

Tweezers and scissors

These can be used for removing projects from the mats. They are also used for removing any excess or negative material like the inside of an O or R. A pair of needle nose scissors gets into tight spaces when just a snip is needed.

Transfer Tape

This is used to move or transfer cut and weeded vinyl to the project surface. You may want to purchase strong grip transfer tape. This works for things like glitter vinyl which doesn't work as well with the regular transfer tape.

Glue

You may need several types of glue like spray adhesive, glue pens or glue dots depending on the project you're working on.

Weeding Tools

Come in several shapes and sizes. They are used to remove the negative material from cut projects especially vinyl.

Cricut Bright Pad

This is a light box that you can set projects on and then illuminate them from underneath. It can make tracing or weeding much easier. There are other, cheaper, options for light boxes available on Amazon.

Iron or Heat Press

If you make vinyl projects that you place on T-shirts you'll need an iron to attach them. If you're doing a lot of shirts a heat press is better but they are usually $150 dollars and up.

Cricut Easy Press

Cricut has recently released a new product called the Cricut Easy Press. Users have mentioned that it's not an actual heat press but more of a large square iron. It retails for around $149.

Though this will work for those doing personal projects it doesn't replace a heat press if you do a lot of projects professionally. It is more portable than a heat press if you want to take it to craft shows or have limited space in your craft room.

Computer Printers

A popular feature in Design Space is sending an image to a computer printer to print and then through the Cricut to cut. This is good if you want to create brightly colored images with a lot of detail.

Some have started their own custom decal and sticker business since any piece of artwork can now be reproduced in DS.

You can use an inkjet or laser printer. However, if you're printing on vinyl or sticker material, a laser printer is not recommended. It uses heat to print and you don't want any sticky residue damaging the printer.

With the Print and Cut feature a good color printer makes all the difference. Here are some recommendations I've seen others make.

Canon Pro 100-S

Canon MX 922

Epson WF-7520

Epson WF-7610

HP Envy 5660

HP OfficeJet Pro 8610

HP PhotoSmart D110

Cricut will keep you informed by email of new accessories as they become available. Talk to users in Facebook groups to find out if they're finding the accessories worth the money. There are also YouTube videos available reviewing new products.

Chapter Thirty Eight – Fixing Frustrating Error Messages

With the introduction of the Cricut Mini the Provo Craft company went in a totally different direction. This little die cutter required the use of a computer and an Internet connection to the Cricut Craft Room to function. Unlike the previous standalone machines where the use of a computer was completely optional.

The entire series of Explore machines require a computer and a reliable high-speed Internet connection to connect to the cloud based Design Space. Gone are the days that you could just pop in a cartridge, select an image and cut it out without the help of any software.

Tip: If you own an older Cricut machine do not get rid of it. It's great to have a backup for those times when you can't complete a project with Design Space.

If you are experiencing problems your Internet service provider may be having issues. The common response from the technician in my area is to reboot my equipment. Well Design Space is no different. Here are six simple fixes to try.

1. With some error messages you can disregard them and hit Continue or just try again by refreshing the browser.

2. The easiest fix is to log out of DS wait a few minutes and log back in.

3. You may want to log in with a different browser. (Do not use Internet Explorer)

4. The next thing to try is to exit from the Cricut Bridge in your system tray at the bottom right-hand corner of your screen next to

the clock. Show your hidden icons and right click the Cricut icon and hit Exit.

5. The last basic troubleshooting technique is to clear your browser's history, cache, cookies and restart the computer before logging back in.

6. Instead of logging in from the shortcut on your desktop or the Cricut Bridge go to your Cricut.com account and access Design Space from there.

Tip: If Windows has done an update or your browser has updated you may experience problems. Completely uninstall all previous versions of DS and reinstall it.

Have you noticed that at certain times of the day DS gives you nothing but trouble? At peak hours when the demand is high your Internet signal may fluctuate causing Design Space to malfunction. You can test your Internet speed and see if you're meeting the minimum requirements which are 1.0 Mbps upload and 1.5 Mbps for download.

Your service provider will have a test page or you can just search for a free test site. If your speeds are below normal call you provider to make sure they are delivering the speed your package promised. You want what you paid for when you signed up.

Besides your ISP an outdated, corrupt or poorly configured web browser, Adware or Spyware, the amount of RAM, CPU processor speed, the operating system and a cable modem can have a negative effect on the ability of your computer to communicate with the Design Space servers. Satellite Internet service has its own unique problems.

I'm not trying to sound like a negative Nelly I just want to give you enough information to know what you're up against; sometimes it's not your fault that DS just doesn't work. My heart goes out to those poor souls who have paying customers waiting for their order to be delivered and the machine owner has to explain the order will be delayed due to technical difficulties not their own.

And last but not least when you're experiencing problems try connecting directly to your computer using your USB cord. I know it's not what all you lovers of wireless technology want to hear but if you're desperate, try the suggestion and see if it helps.

Now in this chapter I'm going to help reduce your down time by explaining the typical error messages you may see when working with Design Space. Earlier I mentioned simple fixes that often resolve the problem. If you've tried those suggestions and it didn't fix the problem here are more specific instructions to follow.

Tip: If you've contacted customer service and they are not able to resolve the problem ask to speak to a technician. They are specifically trained to remotely access your computer and solve the issue.

Plug-in Errors

If you're downloading the Design Space plug-in for the first time make sure that the browser you're using has plug-ins enabled.

Every time Designs Space releases a new version it should update automatically. You should see it updating when you log in.

You can access Design Space by logging into your Cricut.com account or at design.cricut.com. When you download the plug-in just follow the prompts and make sure you **Run as Administrator**.

You should see the Cricut shortcut icon on your desktop when the installation is complete. You'll also see the Cricut Bridge running in your system tray.

But what do you do if the plug-in fails to install properly? If you've had problems before the safe thing to do is delete all old versions before installing the new plug-in. Just go to the downloads folder and get rid of all the old versions then restart your computer.

The operating system may be preventing the downloaded exe file from running on the computer. Once the download is complete and you attempt to click Run and nothing happens here's how to unblock it. Find the file on your desktop or in the downloads folder and right-click it and select Properties. Under the General tab look for the Unblock button click it then click Apply and close the window. Retry the file it should now run successfully.

Here are some common plug-in errors you may encounter.

Design Space is in use exit running Cricut application from the task bar. Right click on the Cricut Bridge in the taskbar next to the clock and select exit. To double check click the start menu and type in Task Manager and select view running processes in Task Manager. Look for CricutBridge.exe select it and hit End Process.

If you switch back and forth from your computer to your mobile device exit out of the iOS or Android App as well.

Error copying files from packed archive. Antivirus software may be causing this problem. Uninstall the plug-in and restart your computer. Then temporarily disable the software until you have downloaded and installed the plug-in. At that point enable or turn the anti-virus software back on.

You may also encounter this error when Windows has done an update. Ignoring the error message and close it. Log out of Design Space wait a few minutes and log back in. If the problem persists uninstall the plug-in then restart your computer and try downloading the plug-in again.

Tip: Adding the Cricut software to a list of programs lets the Windows firewall and antivirus programs know the new software is safe. Add it to a safe list, exclusions or exceptions.

Bypassing Windows Firewall. Windows firewall may be blocking DS installation. Click on Start and type in allow firewall. Select Allow program through Windows Firewall. Look for cricutbridge.exe it should be checked off if not click on Allow another program and search for it and click Add when you find it.

Plug-in is damaged unable to open corrupt file. This is caused when there is a conflict with the security and privacy settings on a Mac. The computer doesn't recognize the unidentified developer. Change the settings, download and install the plug-in and reset the settings. Just click on the Apple icon and select System Preferences. Look for the Security and Privacy icon and click it. At the bottom of the pop-up window you'll see a padlock which will let you make changes when clicked. It will ask for your name and password. Allow applications downloaded from anywhere.

When starting a new project you're prompted to install the plug-in again. DS has had several updates that cause confusion when there are so many versions of the plug-in on your computer. Log out and then get rid of all older versions of the plug-in you download. Then try one or all of the 6 simple fixes mentioned earlier.

Design Space Errors

Power on you Cricut machine and connect it to your computer. When you're Mac, PC, browser or mobile device receives a system update settings can be reset, changed or deleted and you may encounter this error message.

When you set up your Explore for the first time connect it to the computer with the USB cord. After registering your Explore the computer should recognize the device. If not there may be a problem with your drivers. In the Video Tutorials Chapter look for the step-by-step tutorial to help a computer recognize the Explore machine and fix the drivers.

No Cricut device found. Sometimes Bluetooth settings change for a variety of reasons. Check to see if Bluetooth is still turned on under your settings. If you're using the adapter make sure it's securely inserted into the USB port. Unpair by deleting the device and pair it again as you did originally and restart your computer. Make sure your Bluetooth drivers have been updated.

Unable to connect to your machine. When you connect your Explore to the computer using the USB port, all the needed drivers should automatically install. If the drivers fail to install properly Design Space won't be able to find your Explore machine. Go to the Start menu and type in device manager click on it and you should see a list that includes the Explore machine. Right click on it and Update Driver Software. You're going to manually install the drivers select browse my computer for drivers and type in %APPDATA% browse for the AppData folder expand it click Roaming then Design Space then Explore. Finally click Okay.

You should see the full path of all the folders you just selected hit Next and the driver should install properly now.

When the process completes restart your computer. Log back into Design Space and it should now connect to your machine. Visit the Video Tutorial Chapter if you want a step-by-step walkthrough of this process.

Project can't be saved. Does your project contain text? All of your system fonts will automatically show up and DS but not all of them are compatible. When designing with some system fonts which are already loaded on your computer, tablet or phone these can prevent the project from being saved. You can either redesign your project using a different font or try this quick fix. Insert a simple shape like a triangle or square into your design and save the project. Remember to hide that shape layer before you cut the design.

Some free fonts or ones you purchase from an outside source may never show up in Design Space because of their incompatibility the program will not import them.

Remove exclusive content. Try the quick fixes mentioned earlier in this chapter they have resolved problems for me more times and I can count. Naming a project with copyright or licensing terms may trigger this message. See if renaming the project helps. Check to see if you are using new images from an expired Access membership.

Did you close the firmware update window when you logged into DS instead of updating? Performing routine maintenance helps eliminate problems but sometimes we just don't feel like messing with it and we ignore the suggestions. It might just solve your problem.

Firmware update error. When the Internet connection times out or is interrupted before the update is completed, you'll get this error message. Click Retry or access the firmware update from the main menu. To prevent any connection issues don't try updating using Bluetooth use your USB connection instead.

The project contains fonts not found on your computer. This is a typical error message triggered by shareable files. If the shared file you're trying to access was created with a system font you do not have installed on your computer it will trigger this missing content message.

Send to mat unsuccessful. A problem occurred while sending your project to the mat. If your Internet signal is weak or slow try clicking Okay or Continue and repeat the process, sometimes all it needs is another try. If you're using Bluetooth, make sure it's working properly and is up-to-date. If the problem is reoccurring, you might want to connect via USB cable instead.

The API is down. If you have tried several times to sign into Design Space unsuccessfully and finally get the above-mentioned error message click on the main menu. Go to the bottom of the drop down menu and select your country. You should now be able to work successfully in Design Space.

404-HTTP error message. The computer can't find Design Space because the session has timed out or expired. Check to see if you have lost your connection and have to sign in again. Don't be surprised if you can't find the project you're working on you may have to start again. If your Internet connection times out repeatedly get in the habit of saving your projects from time to time so they're not completely lost.

Expected Identifier error message. This is a JavaScript error you'll see when using Internet Explorer. This browser is no longer compatible with Design Space. Try one of these browsers instead. Mozilla Firefox, Google Chrome, Microsoft Edge or Apple Safari.

Grayed out mat. When you hit the Make It button the mat is gray and nothing happens. Try clicking the refresh button on your browser to send the command again.

Page not responding. When the design process is interrupted, and you can't complete a project because it freezes make it easier for Design Space to function. Do not have multiple tabs open in your browser. Close out any other programs. Photoshop for example is a notorious hog when it comes to resources. Hopefully your Internet upload and download speeds meet the minimum requirements for DS.

Page never loads. When the green wheel just spins log out of DS and exit the Cricut Bridge wait a few minutes and log back in with a different browser. If it happens again try refreshing the browser first before forcing a refresh by hitting the Ctrl and F5 button at the same time on the keyboard for Windows and Cmd + R on a Mac.

Disc is full. This error message will pop up in DS when your computer's memory is insufficient to complete the task. Close any unnecessary programs that may be running in the background to boost RAM temporarily. There are additional things you can do like uninstall an old program that's no longer used, disable unused ports, defrag your computer, etc. Just do a Google search for increase RAM, clear memory or how to free up memory to find additional suggestions.

Help with Print and Cut problems

For the Explore and Explore One machine to print and cut accurately it needs to be calibrated. The Explore Air and Air 2 come pre-calibrated from the factory. You can recalibrate any machine that's having trouble cutting printed images correctly. (Calibration PDF included in the User Manual Chapter.)

Also in DS from the mat when you hit Continue you have to select the Send to Printer option. The pop-up printer window lets you find the printer you want to use so you can select it.

Tip: When you use more than one printer one may be set as the default. If you send your project to the printer and nothing happens make sure you're sending it to the correct printer. From the start menu select devices and printers. Right-click the printer and see if it's set as default. Sometimes the same printer can show up twice which will cause confusion.

Printable image is too large. The maximum Print and Cut size used to be 6.25 x 8.75. With the latest update the new size is now 6.75 x 9.25. If you get this error message and all you want to do is cut the image then change the printer icon to the scissors icon in the layers panel. Or resize the image.

Machine cannot read cut sensor marks. With the recent update hopefully we'll see this error message less often. The three L-shaped sensor marks have been replaced by a solid rectangle surrounding the image which should be easier to read.

Older suggestions were to darken the sensor marks with a black magic marker or cover up the marks with scotch tape. And avoid overhead lighting interfering with the sensor by closing the lid. Make sure the Smart Set dial is set on the same material you're working with.

Use white paper. Set your printer settings to letter 8.5 x 11 and best print quality. Don't select shrink to fit or fit to page it needs to print at actual size.

Tip: Make sure there is plenty of black ink in the printer so the registration marks print nice and dark for the sensors to recognize.

Images print off the paper. The computer screen resolution may cause the text and images to print larger than you want. Right click on your desktop and select Screen resolution. Click on Make items larger or smaller and select the default 100%. Click Apply and restart the computer.

Tip: Image files need to be extracted from folders before their uploaded. PDF files can't be uploaded. Export the images inside to upload.

Cutting pauses. The cutting process starts but then stops. When working with complicated projects or making many repeated cuts the Explore machine needs time to process the command. It may pause for a moment and then continue cutting or it stops completely.

It can time out, especially when using Bluetooth. If you're using a mobile device try working closer to your machine to ensure proper communication. Don't have multiple tabs open on the browser or other programs running in the background. If the cutting project can be divided into smaller groups try that. You can always connect with a USB cord to finish the project.

Unsupported image type. The uploaded SVG file contains elements that are not supported. It will ask you to import anyway. Click to Continue and sometimes the file will upload. When it doesn't here's what to do.

If you created the image you can remove the unsupported items like gradients, patterns, edible text, linked images or a clipping mask. Now Design Space can separate your image into layers. If you have no idea how the image was created then you'll have to convert it into a PNG or JPEG. The layers will be lost but at least you'll have a usable image.

Blacklisted item may not be purchased. Some images offered for sale by Cricut may not be purchased in every country due to licensing agreements. When trying to buy an image from the Marvel, Sesame Street or the Anna Griffin collection and others you may receive an unsuccessful purchase error.

Chapter Thirty Nine – Helpful Troubleshooting Techniques

In this chapter I'm going to talk about a few of the problems users have with their machines and discuss ways to solve them. Or better yet to prevent possible problems before they happen with these helpful hints.

Problems with printing images

The Explore machine will work with a variety of printers but some printers will jam when using card stock. The best option is to use a printer that feeds the card stock from the rear. The less turns the card stock makes in the printer the less chance of it jamming.

Play it safe and don't use a laser printer for vinyl or sticky material. The heat of the printer will melt the material and could damage the printer.

Design Space has a printable area that is 6.75 by 9.25. This is a lot bigger than past versions.

When you're working with an image you're going to print you can select a square from the Shapes tool and place it behind your image. Make the size of the square 6.75 and 9.25. Then you can clearly see while you're working with you image whether or not it is within the printable area. Make the square a light color so you can see it separate from your image.

You can put more than one image in the box. Attach the images so you can move them all at one time. Delete the box before printing.

It's easier than ever to create custom designs for multiple uses just by changing their Line type instead of redesigning the whole project.

Pens

When you're inserting a pen into your machine, place a piece of scrap paper under the pen. This keeps the pen from marking up your material or your machine when you click it into the clamp.

There are several ways to breathe new life into dried markers sometimes just soaking the tip will work or refilling the pen with 90% alcohol. (See the Video Tutorial Chapter.)

Besides the homemade universal pen adapter I mentioned, the tube shaped pencil grips fit some markers making them compatible with the Explore.

Problems with cutting images

Before unloading the mat try to determine if the material has been cut to satisfaction. If not manually hit the cut button on the Explore and cut it again several times.

Use the Custom Material Settings in Design Space to increase or decrease the pressure, add multiple cuts, choose an intricate cut setting, or change materials. Within each category there are several listing for different kinds of paper or card stock for example. Just try selecting a different kind and see if that helps.

Tip: Create your own custom settings for any material by selecting Manage Custom Materials from the main menu. Then just click Add New Material and enter the information.

Some complex designs won't cut well in Fast Mode so just cut it regularly. Make sure the blade and mat are clean.

If your images are not cutting correctly be sure and wipe the mat and scrape off any access material left from previous projects. If the mat is severely scored or gouged replace it.

Try switching to another mat such as the stickier blue mat. If the mat isn't sticky enough the material can slip and won't cut properly. Or tape the paper to the mat.

Then carefully clean the blade. If there is still a problem it might be time to replace the blade. Using the new German Carbide blade is your best option for optimal cutting. Believe it or not there can be a slight difference in the cutting edge between one new blade and another.

Make sure the blade fits tightly in the housing. Regularly clean out the blade housing of fibers that accumulate and interfere with the cutting process. Blow into the housing or use a straightened paperclip and carefully loosen and stuck material.

Since the angle of the deep cutting blade is different try using it on regular material when experiencing problems.

If you get a message saying image is too large you simply need to resize the image to make it smaller. Some people think that since the mat is 12 x 12 they can use 12 x 12 images. But there is a slight space left for margins so the largest image size is 11.5 x 11.5. You can purchase a 12 x 24 mat to make larger cuts of 11.5 x 23.5.

If all else fails try a different material. Some users find that certain brands of paper or card stock work better than others.

Mats

If your mat is too sticky when it's new place a white T-shirt on it and press lightly or just pat it with your hands. This will reduce some of the stickiness.

When using a brayer and thin paper don't apply a lot of pressure on the mat. This makes it hard to remove without ripping the paper.

Always clean your mat after each use. Use a scraper to remove small bits of lint or paper that have been left behind. These small scraps will cause problems with future projects.

You can wipe the mat with a damp cloth. Then replace the plastic cover between uses to prevent dust and dirt from sticking to the mat.

When the mat has lost its stickiness; tape the material to the mat around the edges or wash it with a little soap and water, rinse, let dry and it's good to go.

Have you seen those food grade flexible cutting mats or boards? Some users are turning them into Cricut mats. Look for the thin plastic ones that are 12 x 12 or 12 x 24.

Use spray adhesive and cover the mat leaving a border so the glue doesn't get on the rollers or just spray the back of the card stock to adhere to the makeshift mat.

Load and unload

When you load the mat into the Explore always make sure that it's up against the roller wheels and under the guides. This assures the material will load straight when you press the load button.

When the cut is complete never pull the mat out of the machine as this can damage the wheels. Always hit the unload button and then remove the mat.

To extend the life of the mat turn it around and load it from the bottom edge. Position the images on different parts of the mat instead of always cutting in the upper left corner.

Curling

Here's how to avoid curling material into a useless mess. When working with new mats they tend to hold on for dear life.

When you're pulling a project off the mat, do not pull the paper (or whatever material) up and away from the mat. This will cause it to curl into a mess.

Instead turn the mat over and curl it downward. Pull the mat away from the paper instead of pulling the paper up and away from the mat.

It seems like a slight difference but it will save you from trying to uncurl and flatten a project. Just remember how curled the mat was when you first unboxed it had to wait till it flattened out.

Blades

When cutting adhesive material, glue accumulates on the blades and should be periodically removed. Dip a Q-Tip in nail polish remover to clean any sticky residue build up. Check the cutting edge for nicks and that the tip is still intact.

Note: These blades are extremely sharp. Always use the utmost care when removing them or replacing them into your Cricut.

Never leave them lying within reach of children. Save the tips and cap the blades before trashing them.

For best results use the German Carbide blades. The regular Cricut blades will fit in the Explore blade housing even though they're shaped differently.

At this time there is no German Carbide deep cut blade for the Explore. The blade that comes with the deep cut housing for the Explore is the regular deep cutting blade.

Materials

When you're planning a project with a new material it's good to do a small test first to make sure the material cuts the way you want. This will save you from potential problems and from wasting a large amount of material.

Try one of the in-between settings on the Smart Set Dial. Some card stock is thicker than other types so you may need to adjust settings, use the multi cut settings or re-cut the image manually by hitting the cut button again.

By default the Smart Set dial for paper, vinyl, iron-on, card stock, fabric, poster board has been set up to work best with Cricut products. Each material has three settings on the dial. If the cuts aren't deep enough, increase the pressure or decrease the pressure if the cuts are too deep. For even more control use the custom settings within Design Space.

Additionally using a deep cutting blade (with the housing) or adjusting the stickiness of the mat may help.

Iron-on Vinyl

Sometimes the iron on vinyl sticks to the iron. First, be sure your iron is not too hot. Follow the recommendations on the product. Make sure you purchased the type of vinyl that can be applied with an iron not a professional heat press.

Next, try using parchment paper, Teflon sheet or a piece of cotton fabric between the vinyl and the iron. Use a firm heat resistant surface such as a ceramic tile or wooden cutting board to place your project on. Press and hold instead or ironing back and forth.

Always flip the image in Design Space. Put the vinyl shiny side down while cutting and shiny side up when attaching to the material.

Iron-on Glitter Vinyl

When working with glitter vinyl I move the dial one notch passed iron-on vinyl toward light card stock. It seems to cut better using that setting.

After you make the first cut do not remove the mat from the machine. Check to see if it cut through the vinyl, sometimes I have to run it through one more time for a complete cut. Especially if it's a new brand I haven't worked with.

Saving Money on Vinyl

Local sign shops use a lot of vinyl in big rolls. They don't however have much use for the scraps or remnants. They may be willing to sell you a bag cheaply or even give it away. It never hurts to ask.

Tip: Sign vinyl is usually thicker than craft vinyl so make the needed adjustment when cutting.

Stencils

There are many materials you can use to make stencils. Some users suggested plastic file folders that can be found cheaply at a Dollar Store. Another option is sending laminating sheets through a laminating machine and then putting them through your Cricut to cut the stencil. Run it through twice to make sure cuts are complete.

Problems with machine pausing

If your Cricut machine stops while cutting, writing or scoring I've already made several suggestions to correct the problem here's another option.

It maybe the project itself if it always happens try deleting that project and recreating it. Turn off your computer and disconnect from your machine. Turn off your Cricut machine and wait a few moments. Then restart and reconnect.

Problems with scoring or writing

A loose accessory clamp will affect performance. If the scoring tool or pen is shaky or lose, you'll need to make some repairs to the accessory housing. A detailed repair guide is available in the User Manual Chapter.

If your images are not written correctly make sure you are using a pen that is compatible with Cricut. If the pen is unstable try wrapping duct tape around the pen until it is held securely.

Don't try to force markers that are too big into the pen adapter it will crack and you'll have to buy a new one.

Problems with firmware updates

When you first set up the machine your firmware was updated. But from time to time a firmware update is required to help the Explore work smoothly with your computer to enhance performance and add new features. You will be automatically prompted to perform an update just follow the instructions on the screen till you see that the update was successful then you may continue working.

The process should proceed smoothly. However, if you encounter a problem here are a few suggestions. If you tried the update from a mobile device and encountered difficulties try updating from a computer or laptop.

Cricut Explore and Explore One must be updated using a USB cord. Explore Air and Air 2 can be updated using Bluetooth. But you run the risk that the connection may be lost during the upload so use the USB cord.

Make sure your browser is up to date or try a different one.

When the update fails to complete the power button will stay red indicating there is a problem. Log back into Design Space and manually perform the update. Click on the main menu and select Update Firmware then follow the prompts.

If you have more than one Explore machine make sure to select the right one from the drop-down menu. For additional troubleshooting advice don't forget to check out the chapter on User Manuals.

Problems with Bluetooth wireless

If you're using an Explore Air or Explore Air 2 your Cricut machine is already Bluetooth enabled. But with an Explore or Explore One you will need to buy a Bluetooth adaptor.

When using Bluetooth be sure your machine is within in close proximity, no more than 15 feet from of the computer.

Make sure to verify your computer is Bluetooth enabled. If not, you'll need to buy a Bluetooth Dongle and place it in an unused USB port.

If you lose the Bluetooth connection, try uninstalling your Cricut under Bluetooth devices and then reinstalling.

Some people find their Design Space software works faster by using the USB cord instead of the Bluetooth connection.

Problems with Design Space

Providing your Internet connection is secure and running at top speed, completely logging out of DS and exiting the Cricut Bridge solves a multitude of problems.

Reread the simple fixes in Chapter Thirty Eight or find the solution to a specific error message.

Updating the DS plugin should be automatic when there is a new version.

If a problem occurs check to see if Design Space is up to date. Hover over the Cricut Bridge to see the version number and ask customer service if that's the latest update.

Problems when linking cartridges to Design Space

You've tried to link the cartridge but something went wrong. Instead of seeing the cartridge successfully linked message nothing happens or you'll get these error messages telling you that the cartridge was already linked, can't be recognized or the machines is in use.

Providing you completed the Explore machine setup successfully, have the latest Firmware update, are logged in on a computer, are using an unlinked cartridge, try refreshing your browser for a simple fix. You may have to clear the browser's history, cache and cookies as well.

For a more aggressive approach sign out of Design Space. Remove the cartridge and turn off the Explore. Disconnect the USB cord and wait a few minutes before rebooting the computer. Connect the Explore to the computer once it has completely restarted, sign back into Design Space and try again.

Some cartridges have specific issues that require assistance. If you've done everything you can to resolve the problem don't hesitate to contact customer support. It might not be your fault.

Call or use the live chat feature on the cricut.com page. If you registered the cartridge customer support should have that information if not have a copy of your receipt and a photo of the cartridge ready to provide proof of ownership.

Don't hesitate to contact customer support to get help with your problems. Calling and speaking to a live person gets better results than chatting. The customer service team does its best to handle the situation. For unresolved problems ask to speak to a technician who has been trained with the technical knowledge you need.

Customer care: 877-7CRICUT M-F 9 a.m. – 8 p.m. EST

Chapter Forty – Making Money with Your Cricut

Crafting can be costly. There is the expense of your machine, paper, card stock, vinyl, pens and other accessories. Because of this, several users have asked me if I have any suggestions for making money with the Cricut. They would like to offset their costs and make a little spending cash.

What better way to make some extra money than doing something you love? Here are some ideas. For a ton of selling suggestions check out my Craft Vinyl book.

Selling Crafts

First, of course, is simply selling the crafts you make. One option is local craft shows and fairs. The best way to do this is to come up with your own unique ideas for products.

Also, think outside the box regarding fairs. Don't just attend craft fairs where you'll be competing against others creating the same old things.

For example, at a trade show for new parents you can sell growth charts and personalized baby book covers, wall decorations, blankets, or clothing. At a bridal show you can advertise invitations, guest books or photo album covers.

You can also set up a store online on your own website or through an Etsy store. A Facebook business page is another option. It costs nothing to set-up, but you can pay to run ads that draw people to your page.

The hard part of selling crafts is that you not only have to cover the cost of your materials but also allow for your time. Because many crafters spend a lot of time on their projects it's hard to recoup the value of their time.

Before setting your prices, visit fairs and online stores. Find out what other crafters are charging for the items you want to sell. You may find that the market value is not high enough to pay for your supplies and your time. By doing your research in advance you can find which projects are worth pursuing.

You may be able to cut costs by carefully shopping for materials and buying in bulk for items you use a lot. For additional savings at Cricut.com check out the items under Sale which include clearance, bulk supplies and material bundles.

Talk to owners of local stores who buy and sell local art. They may be willing to buy your projects wholesale or put them in their store on a commission basis.

Personalized items make great gifts

Personalization is the key to your Cricut crafts. You can take a low-cost set of glasses that you buy at a department store and add a family name or initials and sell them for much more than you paid for them.

Local sports teams and clubs are often potential customers. They want T-shirts and items with their logo but they don't want to buy in large quantities as some companies demand for specialized orders.

Another popular market for personalized clothing is items for children with their name or favorite animal images. Grandparents are an especially good target market.

Book clubs might like the name of their club on book bags for all their members to carry.

Organizations might like their logo on mugs or shirts to be sold for a fundraiser.

Apparel and other fabric items can be personalized using Heat Transfer Vinyl. This adhesive vinyl adheres to fabric. It can be purchased in rolls or sheets. Practically any image can be created in DS and applied to the fabric using a heat press or iron.

Note: Don't sell items using images covered under copyright laws featuring Professional Sports Teams or Cartoon Characters.

Teaching Classes

There's a whole industry based on home parties. Now you can be the queen of Cricut parties!

Many people buy their Cricut machines but then have trouble mastering their use. You could teach a small class in your home where you demonstrate how to make a few simple crafts and cover the basics. Then you create a more advanced class for specialized projects.

If you want to have room for more students, you may be able to rent a room cheaply at a library or community center and hold a class there. You can simply demonstrate how to create projects and work in Design Space or you can have participants bring their own machines and laptops or iPads. Check to be sure free Wi-Fi is available.

Charging $20 for a three-hour class and having 15 students will result in a gross profit of $300.

You could also have kits available for certain projects where you gather all the materials and divide them into packets. Sell these kits for a little more than you bought the material for making a small profit.

It saves buyers time by having everything together in one place and ready to go. They won't have to drive all over town to craft stores or spend time online searching for the right type of vinyl or card stock. Plus, they won't have to buy a large packet of materials for one project. You're doing all the prep work for them.

Ask your students what they're having trouble with or what they'd like to learn and develop more classes around those suggestions. People love to gather together and share their passion for arts and crafts.

All my Cricut books are available in paperback have a supply on hand to help your students.

Another class option is a Mom and Me class. Mothers (or dads) bring their child with them and learn to make a craft together. This could be popular with Boy's and Girl's clubs, Scout Troops or even non-profit organizations.

Blogging and YouTube videos

Many crafters are starting blogs and YouTube channels around Cricut products. But how do they make money you ask? They may sell projects and design ideas or images if they're an artist.

But mostly they make money through affiliate sales. To do this go to **Shareasale.com** and sign up to be an affiliate. You can then post links to Cricut products on your blog. If someone clicks through and purchases products from your blog you get a commission on the sale.

A good way to bring people to your blog is by making YouTube videos. Show and explain how to do a project on your Cricut or explain how you solved a problem you were having in Design Space. Then share a link to your blog. Publish a disclosure notice on your blog that explains you receive commissions from affiliate sales.

You may also ask people to sign-up for your mailing list by offering some sort of incentive such as a video course or free image files.

Then you can email your list when new items become available. Don't try to sell something in every email. Offer value to your readers so they keep opening and reading your emails and don't unsubscribe from your list.

But when you do have something to sell you already have a warm market of buyers who trust you. Then you simply send out an email and watch payments pop into your PayPal account.

You can manage a free email list through a site like https://www.mailerlite.com/invite/fdae1f6d44785

Facebook groups are a popular way to get in contact with like-minded people. Join or start your own group and post videos and answer questions that other members have. Again, you can sell affiliate products through links on your own page.

These are just a few ways you can make some extra money with your Explore. The sky's the limit so use your imagination!

Chapter Forty One – How to Video Tutorials

I love YouTube it's a great resource whenever I want to learn something new or find a solution to a nagging problem. I can usually find videos that answer my questions.

Did you know you can download videos and watch them offline anytime you want?

Until recently you could download directly from YouTube by clicking the option it would automatically download to your desktop. Then all you had to do was click on the thumbnail and it would play in Windows Media Player.

Now the cool feature seems to have disappeared, hopefully it will come back. Instead there are websites that will download YouTube videos or playlist's for you. Just do a search for download YouTube videos if that option appeals to you.

It's like having a teacher guiding you each step of the way through your projects. You can work on Design Space from your computer and have a mobile device set up next to it playing the videos you need.

Even though some of these videos feature Design Space 2 the information is still useful.

Cricut Print Then Cut in Design Space

https://youtu.be/eL6kE4TjupA

Working with custom settings

https://youtu.be/Du4nvhAi7XU

Cricut Design Space - Slice, Attach, Weld, Flatten, Contour

https://youtu.be/j5OcuFZo90Y

Write and Cut with Cricut Explore

https://youtu.be/Xnlur1VO8KQ

Creating Oversized Images in Design Space

https://youtu.be/mKQYanQLOh8

iPad App tutorial

https://youtu.be/bfK6CzLOdp8

How to cut your photos into cute shapes

https://youtu.be/VoO8JHMH8xk

Creating words into shapes

https://youtu.be/wUbccPItUj0

Cutting Vinyl sheets without a mat

https://youtu.be/dz4MwfDFjzY

Official iron-on vinyl (T-shirt template now available)
https://youtu.be/uF7uw3wb5xQ

How to curve text in Design Space letter by letter

https://youtu.be/E5eUoW3sXFA

How to curve text for Design Space using Microsoft Word

https://youtu.be/AJTRWxA_dKY

Fixing Cricut Explore Drivers

https://youtu.be/lxgNxdEr3yI

Chapter Forty Two – Practical FAQ's

Accessories

1. What are Cricut mystery boxes? Every month Cricut puts together a treasure trove of products and makes them available to you. It's a surprise what's inside you never know what you'll get until it arrives in the mail. The price varies but you always get more than you pay for. Like paying 30 bucks for products valued at more than $125.

2. I bought of Cricut cartridge from a craft store. I registered the cartridge but can't find it in Design Space. Is it a bootleg cartridge? Did I get ripped off? No. Registering and linking are two different things. When you buy physical cartridges they have to be linked to your account before they'll show up in Design Space.

3. Do all physical cartridges have a digital version available for sale? No. Not all physical cartridges have been made available as a digital cartridge. Some digital cartridges don't have a physical version either. Even though the physical version is no longer available it still may be for sale as a digital cartridge only.

4. Can I get a refund on a digital image I purchased? Digital images are not usually refundable that's why I suggested working with it in DS to see if it's what you want before purchasing. Ask customer service to help you with the problem you're having with the image or if they will give you store credit.

5. If I link cartridges to Design Space can I still use them in my Cricut Create? Yes. Linked cartridges can still be used in the older Cricut machines.

6. Once a cartridge is linked do I have to insert it into the Explore every time I want to use the images on it? No. Once it is linked all the images on the cartridge are stored in your account and are available in DS.

7. How do I register cartridges? In Design Space click on the main menu either on the Home page or from the canvas and select Account Information. On the right-hand side look for Register Products click it and Add New to fill in the information.

8. What accessories should I buy? This is dependent on the types of projects you make and your personal preference. It will take some trial and error to determine what you need. Discussions with other crafters will also be helpful.

9. Should I buy a value pack when I purchase my machine? These packs can be cost effective if you know you'll use the items that are included. Check the prices of the item if purchased separately to see how much money you'll save.

10. How can I save money on accessories? One of the best ways to save money on accessories is not to buy anything until you have a specific purpose for it. It's easy to get carried away and buy things that you then find you don't need or want.

Also, don't think you have to buy everything from Cricut. As we discussed in Chapter Eight there are many pens compatible with your machine that are much cheaper. I gave you a list in that chapter. This is also true of items such as scissors and tweezers. A trip to the local Dollar Store may provide you with the tools you need at a fraction of the cost.

Account Information

11. I already have a Cricut account should I create a new account for my Explore? No. That way any previously linked cartridges will also be available in Design Space.

12. Can I register used Cricut machines? Yes. Just go to https://design.cricut.com/#/setup when you set up the Explore machine it will automatically register it to your account and you can download the Design Space plugin.

Bluetooth Wireless

13. Do all the Explores have built-in Bluetooth? No. Explore Air and Explore Air 2 have Bluetooth built in. With the Explore and the Explore One you will have to use a USB cord to connect or buy a Bluetooth adaptor.

14. How do I connect my iPhone or iPad to my machine? Turn on your Explore machine. Go to the settings in your phone or tablet. Turn on Bluetooth. Look for Cricut Device on the list of devices your phone or tablet shows. Click on Cricut device.

15. How do I download the Cricut App? Click on the App Store icon. Then type Design Space and it will bring up the App. Click to download and install. You will need to enter your Cricut ID or set one up. When you open the App it will walk you through the steps to attach to a new device.

16. My computer is not Bluetooth enabled do I have to buy a new computer? No. Purchasing a Bluetooth Dongle and inserting it into a USB port on a computer of laptop will enable your machine to communicate with the Explore and let you go wireless.

17. All my USB ports are full now what? A USB hub acts like a power strip freeing up ports by adding several USB ports to your system.

Computers and Devices

18. Can fonts be added to an iPad and iPhone? Yes. The number of fonts available on mobile devices is very limited especially from a designer's standpoint. So third party developers created App's to help users install fonts. There are paid versions like AnyFont or Font Manager which is free. Do your own searches to find other Apps for both iOS and Android that make the installation process easier.

19. Do I have to link cartridges to my mobile devices? No. Cartridges are linked to your Cricut account that way they are available across the entire Cricut platform. Older machines, Cricut Craft Room, the Gypsy and Design Space.

20. Can I upload images to Design Space using a mobile device? Not at this time. There used to be a workaround, but that trick doesn't seem to apply any longer after DS updated. Uploaded images from a computer or laptop are available on the App. Click on the image button on the bottom left which brings up the images. Click on the little funnel icon in the upper right to filter and find uploaded images.

21. Why does Chrome save vector images as a Chrome HTML Document instead of SVG files? In Windows 10 depending on your settings this miscommunication may happen. That is not a file format Design Space recognizes which prevents it from being uploaded. Try to drag and drop the image into DS, use another browser like Firefox, convert the file or change Chrome's settings.

22. I have an iPad, but it didn't automatically update like the Design Space plug-in did. How do I fix the problem? You don't it's not a problem the App will continue to function and update only when needed. The plug-in and the App are two separate programs. The browser plug-in updates routinely.

23. Does Design Space work with a Mac? Yes. It's compatible with Apple products including computers, iPads, iPod Touch and iPhones.

24. Does Design Space work on an Android Device? Yes. The free Android App for Design Space is available at the Google Play Store. As long as your device's operating system is OS 4.4 or later it should work. There are known issues and Cricut encourages user feedback to improve the App. (See the User Manual Chapter for additional info.) It won't work on a Google Chromebook though.

It's currently in beta with limited functions and only available in the U.S. It will continue to be developed as they get the bugs worked out.

25. Can you work with Design Space offline? Yes. Just download the project while you're online. Make sure to include the fonts and images you want to design with so they're available to work with offline on your iPhone or iPad. If you don't have an iOS device check out my Design Space alternatives in the Resource Chapter.

Design Space

26. How much does Design Space cost? It's free. Images and fonts or a subscription to Cricut Access can be purchased or you can use the free images or upload your own.

27. Can I use more than one Explore machine with Design Space? Yes. You can have numerous models registered with one account. Select the model from the drop down box in Design Space when it appears.

28. Can I use my Cricut Explore without Design Space? No. It must be connected to a device such as a computer, phone, or tablet to create projects through the Design Space Software or Apps.

29. Can I subscribe to Cricut Access for a month to see if I like it? Yes. There is a monthly option. It automatically renews every month so you'll have to cancel it if you change your mind. Log into Design Space click on the main menu and select Account Information. Click on Subscriptions and Memberships on the right and find Cricut Access hit the cancel button under Payment Info.

30. What happens to the images I bought during my Cricut access subscription once it expires? Any images or digital cartridges you purchased during your subscription remains available even if you cancel. Once you pay for it remains in Design Space.

31. I just installed a new system font and now my Explore freezes up? Unfortunately some fonts are not compatible in Design Space. Delete the newly installed font then try using another to resume functionality.

32. How can I download images from the DS canvas and save them on my computer? Increase the size of the image. JPEG images get distorted when you try to enlarge them so do it beforehand. The size of the image can always be reduced later if needed. Turn the grid off on the canvas and take a screenshot of the image with the snipping tool.

33. I have a Cricut Expression 2 can I use Design Space? No. Design Space works with Explore machines. The Cricut Craft Room works with all older models like the original little bug Cricut Personal Cutter, Create, Cake, Mini and Expression machines.

34. Is there a multi-cut setting in Design Space? Yes. There's an option to turn the multi-cut function on or off for most materials. When you hit the Make It button on the mat preview screen click Continue select the machine from the drop-down menu and click on Set Material. From the pop-up menu click on view all and scroll to the bottom and click on Material Settings. Select the material and click Edit to make the changes.

35. That sounds complicated is there an easier way? Yes. Manually tell the Explore machine to re-cut the image. Do not unload the mat just hit the Cut button again and the image will re-cut as many times as needed.

Explore Machines

36. Can I try before I buy a Cricut Explore? Maybe. Call craft stores in your area like Joanne's, Michael's or Hobby Lobby to see if they're planning a demo day or have the machine you can use. If not ask them if they know any instructors in the area offering classes.

37. My Explore is making a funny noise can I squirt it with WD-40? No. The machine comes pre-lubed with a layer of grease on the bar the carriages ride on. So be careful when you clean it not to remove too much of the lubricant. Customer service will send out a grease packet when contacted.

38. I'm using the Fast Mode to cut a design but the cuts are imperfect, now what? Humidity affects paper when stored. Try card stock from a new unopened package. If the design is very detailed the Fast Mode should not be used.

39. The Fast Mode is grayed out in Design Space when cutting paper, how do I enable it? The option to use the Fast Mode is not available on all materials. It only works on vinyl through card stock on the Smart Set dial.

Firmware

40. How will I know when to update my Firmware? When you log into Design Space it will tell you if there are updates available for your machine. It will walk you through the process.

Materials

41. Can the Explore cut freezer paper stencils? Yes. Use the custom settings for parchment paper or wax paper.

42. What types of materials can I cut with my Explore? Paper, card stock, canvas, thin cardboard, fabric, metal, vinyl, leather Balsa wood, to see a complete list see the User Manual Chapter.

43. What kind of material do I need for attaching designs to fabric and clothing? Use Heat Transfer Vinyl which goes by other names like Iron-on Vinyl or T-Shirt Vinyl.

44. Do I need stretching vinyl for clothing made out of stretchy material? Yes. It's recommended for best results. When using regular HTV, Heat Transfer Vinyl will start to crack quickly as the material stretches.

45. What kind of material do I need on glassware? The material must be FDA approved for food items for your own safety and that of your customers.

46. Can I cut different kinds of material on the same mat? Yes. That's a good way to use up small scraps of paper or vinyl. Position the images on the mat select them all and hit Attach so they stay in place.

Print and Cut Images

47. Are there any quick fixes to common problems when buying SVG files? Yes. Cutnedgecrafts.com explains what to do. Visit the site and search for the article 5 Common SVG Problems Solved.

48. Does the Print and Cut function require special paper? No. Even cheap notebook paper can be used if you don't mind the quality. Depending on your project quality paper like card stock, Avery labels, matte photo paper, magnet sheets or printable vinyl produce the best results. You can even print specialty paper for quilting, beading, music, games, postcards and CD sleeves and a host of other templates. Just do a search for printable paper or digital paper to find free sources that can be saved as a PDF or JPEG.

49. How does the Explore print images? You choose the Print and Cut option for the images and send them to the printer. Then load the printed images on the mat and follow the on screen prompts in Design Space to cut them out. It's a two-step process since the Explore doesn't actually do the printing.

Writing

50. Where is the option to Write with a Cricut pen instead of cut? The Write icon is located in Design Space on the Layers panel it's one of the attributes on top of the Basic colors panel. You'll need to have a pen in the Explore machine. With the Explore One you'll need to take out the blade housing and replace it with the pen and adaptor.

51. Isn't writing and printing the same thing? No. When you use the writing option it's more of a style. Think of it as decorative handwriting or handwritten script like you do when writing a letter. It's just a single pen line whereas printing will show full letters filled with color.

52. Can you use a Scoring Stylus with the Explore? Yes. You'll need to buy an adaptor and a scoring tool which will emboss as well. Don't confuse it with the Cricut Scoring Tip and Housing for older models.

Chapter Forty Three – Valuable Resources

The first place to go for all your Cricut questions and problems is the official Cricut page at cricut.com. You'll find the latest in machines, designs, accessories and tutorials.

Facebook Groups

There are many Facebook groups for Cricut users that you can join to ask questions and receive answers from other crafters. They also share designs and projects at no cost to each other. Discount coupons are also shared.

When you join a group take a few minutes to read their rules. Most groups will remove anyone without warning that doesn't follow the rules. This can include anything from promoting something to sell or using inappropriate language. Every group is different so take the time to read and follow their rules.

https://www.facebook.com/OfficialCricut/

https://www.facebook.com/groups/LetsLearnCricutExplore/

https://www.facebook.com/groups/937801949607138/

https://www.facebook.com/groups/CricutLoversGuide/

Where to find SVG files

These sites offer free files as well as paid ones. You can visit them frequently to see what they're currently offering for free.

https://apexembdesigns.com/cuttables/cuttables

http://svgcuts.com/blog/

http://digiplayground.com/blog/category/weekly-free-files/

http://www.3dsvg.com/product-category/free-svg-files-cricut-silhouette/?orderby=date

http://svgcuttingfiles.com/catalog.php?category=1

https://www.misskatecuttables.com/products/freebie-of-the-day/

Where to download fonts

Download 10,000 fonts perfect for scrapbooking, crafts, cards, logos, party invitations, newsletters, flyers and more. Compatible for both Windows and Mac's.

http://cricutdiecuttingmachine.com/f.php

http://www.dafont.com/

Where to buy t-shirts

https://www.jiffyshirts.com/

https://www.sassyapparelblanks.com/

http://www.shirtchamp.com/

Search online for live Cricut Events like these or contact events@cricut.com if you can't find one in your area.

https://cricutdallas.splashthat.com/

https://cricuthouston.splashthat.com/

See what other crafters are making:

http://thecuttingcafe.typepad.com/cutting_cafe_blog/cricut-explore/

https://www.creativebug.com/cricut

http://cricuttop40.com/

http://meandmycricut.com

Here's a blog about developing a craft businesses you might find helpful.

http://cuttingforbusiness.com/

Generate word art images at **wordart.com**

There are free vector editing programs like Inkscape, Method Draw, RollApp, Vectr, LibreOffice and Fatpaint. As well as online SVG converters at **pngtosvg.com** or **picsvg.com**.

Cricut Design Space alternatives

Looking for easy to learn offline solutions to Design Space? Sure Cuts a Lot and Make the Cut are both downloadable software that reside on your computer. Once installed no Internet connection or Wi-Fi hotspot is needed.

They create completely compatible cut files you upload into Design Space to cut or print.

http://cricutdiecuttingmachine.com/a.php

Chapter Forty Four – Essential User Manuals

Like I mentioned before Design Space will continue to update. Some of this information uses DS2 screen shots even though DS3 in now available. The information is still useful as long as you keep that in mind. DS2 can be identified by the green Cricut logo in the upper left corner DS3 just says Canvas.

Your Cricut account info

http://help.cricut.com/help/account-faq

Setting up your Explore machine

http://help.cricut.com/sites/default/files/pdfs/01dmachine.pdf

Official Cricut channel

https://www.youtube.com/channel/

UCenmvBlGmukLZG0ELpS6mRQ

Cricut Explore manuals

http://help.cricut.com/help/manuals

http://learn.cricut.com/cricut-explore%C2%AE/

manuals/cricut-explore

http://learn.cricut.com/cricut-explore-one%E2%84%A2/

manuals/cricut-explore-one

http://learn.cricut.com/cricut-explore-air%E2%84%A2/

manuals/cricut-explore-air

Design Space manual

http://learn.cricut.com/design-space%C2%AE/manuals/
design-space-pc/mac-0

How to install Design Space

http://help.cricut.com/help/install-design-space

Helping Cricut Design Space software to connect

http://help.cricut.com/help/cricut-anti-virus-exception

http://help.cricut.com/help/cricut-firewall-exception

Firmware Update for Explore machines

http://help.cricut.com/help/firmware-update-explore

Troubleshooting Firmware update

http://help.cricut.com/help/firmware-update-failing

iOS manual for iPad and iPhone

http://learn.cricut.com/design-space%C2%AE/
manuals/design-space-ios

Setup for iPad or iPhone

https://youtu.be/ILBl9bE3vqc

Paper saving tips for iOS devices

http://help.cricut.com/help/move-hide-iOS

Working offline FAQ's

http://help.cricut.com/faq/design-space-offline

Android App overview

http://learn.cricut.com/cricut-explore-air-2/software-apps/

design-space-android/design-space-beta-android-app-overview

Available at the Google App store for free

https://youtu.be/c7H1v1QmWI0

General FAQ's

http://help.cricut.com/top-answers

http://help.cricut.com/faq/cricut-explore

http://help.cricut.com/faq/cricut-explore-one

http://help.cricut.com/faq/cricut-explore-air

SnapMat FAQ

http://help.cricut.com/faq/snapmat

http://help.cricut.com/sites/default/files/2016-
08/SnapMat%20User%20Manual%20iOS_1.pdf
Understanding the Smart Set dial

http://learn.cricut.com/explore-air-2/machine

Cut settings for different material

http://help.cricut.com/help/cricut-explore-materials-settings

Using custom settings

http://help.cricut.com/help/custom-setting-smart-set-dial

How fast mode works

http://help.cricut.com/help/explore-air-2-fast-mode

Print then cut calibration for Explore and Explore One

(Air and Air 2 come pre calibrated)

http://help.cricut.com/sites/default/files/pdfs/

15calibrationforprintthencut.pdf

http://help.cricut.com/sites/default/files/pdfs/Calibration.pdf

http://help.cricut.com/help/explore-sensor-marks-troubleshooting

http://help.cricut.com/sites/default/files/2016-08/

Calibration_1.pdf

https://youtu.be/2Pg0HXDfWr0

How to link cartridges

http://help.cricut.com/help/cartridge-linking-design-space

http://help.cricut.com/sites/default/files/pdfs/14asingcartridges.pdf

Finding free images that came with the machine

http://help.cricut.com/help/cricut-explore-free-content

Cricut Access subscriptions

http://help.cricut.com/help/subscription-and-memberships

http://help.cricut.com/help/cricut-access

Cartridges in Access plus all 400 with handbook

http://content.cricut.com/b/pdfs/ca_image_library_list.pdf

http://help.cricut.com/cartridge-library

Cricut Basics App

http://help.cricut.com/faq/cricut-basics

http://help.cricut.com/help/design-space-make-it-now-projects

Help with Cricut accessories

http://help.cricut.com/help/accessories

Video overview for pens, scoring tip and blades

http://learn.cricut.com/explore-air-2/supplies

Concluding Words of Encouragement

Before I invested hundreds of dollars in Photoshop, I took a class. The only problem was that I missed the beginner's class and had to take the intermediate one. Needless to say I was apprehensive since I had never worked with Photoshop before.

I'll never forget the first class it was packed. I surprised myself and was able to keep up. I took notes and during the break practiced what I learned the more I practiced the easier it got. I was beginning to understand how Photoshop worked.

After the break there were several empty seats and the teacher said those students became discouraged at how much there was to learn and gave up. They felt overwhelmed and quit the class.

Don't let that happen to you with Design Space. Learn a little or a lot at your own pace. I'm here to help you understand how Design Space works. Soon you'll be proud to say "I mastered Design Space too!"

I had fun writing this book and I feel it's a helpful, timesaving guide for Explore users.

Have you found any of these tips useful? If so please help me get the word out. Mention this Cricut Explore book on your blog, tweet about it, pin it or post comments on your Facebook page.

Check out my new book **Coloring Crafts**

Crazy about coloring have stacks of finished coloring books lying around. What the heck do you do with them? Transform colored pages into home décor, fun gifts, cool clothing or editable art. Coloring crafts will even show you how to turn coloring pages into cash!

About the Author

I'm all about doing things the easy way after all crafting should be fun and easy because when it's not it's too much like work.

So I got in the habit of looking for quick solutions to all those annoying problems I had, trying to figure out how to get the little bug to make all those fantastic cuts since that was the reason I forked over my hard-earned money and bought the silly machine.

I wrote all the tips down and when I couldn't find a solution I experimented until I invented my own problem-solving technique.

I began to think if these tips, tricks and troubleshooting solutions have helped me, maybe they will help other Cricuter's. If you've seen the forums you know Cricut crafters are generous, love to share and are more than willing to help, ergo the reason I wrote these handy guide books.

Thanks for your help and happy crafting.

Maryann Gillespie

Notes

Made in the USA
Columbia, SC
17 December 2019

85125368R00152